ACKNOWLEDGMENTS

My husband, John Douglas Stone, has been a steadfast supporter throughout the doctoral process--shouldering the responsibilities of daily life so that I could be free to pursue my studies.. I dedicate this dissertation to Doug, my best friend and helpmate for twenty-five years.

I thank my parents, Silas and Elsie Bishop of Mobile, Alabama. By their example, I learned tenacity, a sense of responsibility, and a desire for lifelong learning.

I thank Dr. Paul George who has been a calm, steady influence. His generosity in sacrificing time from his sabbatical to support and encourage my studies made the crucial difference. I also want to recognize my other committee members: Dr. Robert Sherman whose care and attention to quality was so valued and respected; Dr. James Hensel who more than any other person gave me practical advice on meeting the demands of the doctoral process; Dr. Robert Myrick whose tremendous service to the counseling profession inspired me to try to produce a product worthy of contribution to the field; and Dr. Phillip Clark whose direction and support contributed greatly to a finished product.

I wish to thank Dr. John Dixon who graciously and generously offered consultation services throughout the

analysis of data. Dr. Linda Crocker, Dr. Robert Drummond
and Dr. David Honeyman provided assistance when it was above
and beyond their call of duty.

I want to offer special recognition to Lorene Gibson,
Mary Ann Dyal, and Mildred Dixon, each of whom acted as
editor, typist, consultant, soundingboard, and friend.

Finally, I thank Timmy Bishop. The miracle of his life
taught me to value and develop every gift.

TABLE OF CONTENTS

LIST OF TABLES

Abstract of Dissertation Presented to the Graduate School
of the University of Florida in Partial Fulfillment of the
Requirements for the Degree of Doctor of Education

MERITOCRACY OF HIGH SCHOOL
MATHEMATICS CURRICULUM PLACEMENT

By

Carolyn Stone

August, 1995

Chairman: Paul George
Major Department: Educational Leadership

This study measured the mathematics gatekeeping

process, the mechanism by which educators assign students to

the critical ninth-grade mathematics courses, against a

meritocratic definition of fairness to determine if this

process denied access to students from particular segments

of society. The gatekeeping process was fair according to

meritocratic principles if factors extraneous to academic

ability were not significantly related to which students

were denied admission to Algebra I and Geometry, the

gatekeeper mathematics courses. While controlling for

academic ability, this study assessed if socioeconomic

status, race, gender, and school assignment taken

independently and in combination were significant in

predicting which students were denied admission to

gatekeeper mathematics courses.

ix

The sample for this study was drawn from a large urban school district and included all the 1993-1994 ninth-grade students who scored in the upper quartile on one of three eighth-grade mathematics standardized tests of achievement. Logistic regression models were used to analyze the data.

Analyses of the data produced the following results: school assignment, socioeconomic status, and the combination of gender and socioeconomic status were significantly related to students being denied admission to gatekeeper mathematics when academic ability was controlled. The findings of this study evinced that students who scored in the upper quartile in mathematics were not scheduled into the gatekeeper mathematics courses without regard to their socioeconomic status, gender, or school assignment. Therefore, the admission of students to gatekeeper mathematics did not adhere to the meritocratic definition of fairness because admission into gatekeeper mathematics was denied for students from particular segments of society.

This study concluded with the recommendation that educators need to understand the issues involved in educational equity and to be able to identify school practices that promote or deter equity. Curriculum enrollment patterns that discourage equitable access must be identified and, more importantly, eliminated.

CHAPTER 1

INTRODUCTION

Education in America traditionally has been viewed as a basic right. Most Americans would say with conviction that education is a high priority in this country and that it serves as a stepping-stone to upward social mobility. High school curriculum programs provide the basis for the differentiation of opportunity within schools, particularly the mathematics curriculum (Gamoran, 1987). Tracking and course selection together account for substantially significant differences in access to higher education (Alexander, Cook, & McDill, 1978). The judgments of guidance counselors and, to a lesser degree, teachers directly affect a student's access to various courses and shape the curriculum paths that a student takes.

The primary "gatekeeper" courses--those that allow students to meet the minimum entrance requirements in mathematics for admission to most four-year postsecondary institutions--are Algebra I or Geometry as a minimum for a ninth-grade student (Commission on Precollege Guidance and Counseling, 1986; Oakes, 1990a). The gatekeeping process normally begins in the spring of the eighth-grade year when a student is assigned to a ninth-grade schedule of courses. Access to the gatekeeper mathematics courses most often is

1

based on academic ability as determined by standardized achievement test scores (Lee & Ekstrom, 1987; Oakes 1990a).

Most secondary schools sort students based upon their academic ability and achievement. Educators deem this type of sorting of students to be meritocratic.

> Education plays an essential role in meritocratic societies. It serves as a sorting agency, where the most talented individuals, no matter what their social class origins, are identified and groomed for further schooling. The most capable high-achieving students go through college. . . . Other students go as far as their talents will take them in school and then take more modest employment. (Webb & Sherman, 1989, pp. 490-491)

The task of assigning students into courses is primarily the responsibility of the guidance counselor. Teachers also may make recommendations, although to a lesser degree. Guidance counselors base their decisions upon an objective record of a student's ability and performance, a record that includes course grades, current schedule of courses, and scores on standardized achievement tests (Lee & Ekstrom, 1987). These test scores are critical in determining admission to the ninth-grade "gatekeeper" mathematics courses. As long as the admissions tests are valid and reliable measures of a student's academic ability and factors extraneous to academic ability are ignored or eliminated with regard to student placement, the gatekeeping process is meritocratic. It continues to be meritocratic if at all subsequent scheduling sessions counselors base their recommendations about the mathematics courses students should pursue upon valid and reliable measures of student academic ability. Factors extraneous to academic ability should be unrelated to course placement in order for the scheduling process to remain meritocratic.

Students' course assignments in high school significantly differentiate their opportunities beyond high school (Oakes, 1990a, 1990b). Assignment to college preparatory mathematics courses allows students the possibility of then pursuing higher education. It is fitting, therefore, from a meritocratic point of view, that students in the basic mathematics tracks typically cannot seek higher education at a four-year institution, although this option is available for students in the college track mathematics courses. "In a meritocracy, justice demands that a student of superior abilities should have superior opportunities" (Brubacher, 1982, p. 65). Secondary schools have upheld their responsibility for providing equal educational opportunity as long as the distribution of educational resources is proportional to the students' relative academic abilities (Brubacher, 1982; Giarelli & Webb, 1980).

On the other hand, critics of meritocracy view the assignment of gatekeeping mathematics courses as inequitable because it aspires to the principle of providing educational opportunities based on academic ability. These critics disagree with the idea that there are valid measures of student academic ability. Instead of determining academic ability, these measures are viewed as stratifiers, contributing to the reproduction and perpetuation of the existing social order (Bowles & Gintis, 1976; Good & Brophy, 1987; Purpel & Shapiro, 1985; Rosenbaum, 1987; Slavin, 1988). The contention is that students of social privilege score higher on standardized assessment measures; therefore, these measures cannot be valid for all students (Bowles & Gintis, 1976; Good & Brophy, 1987; Oakes, 1990b; Wilkerson, 1982). Social privilege, defined in terms of socioeconomic status, race, and gender (McClelland, 1990), leads the critics of meritocracy to question the fairness of the process of assigning gatekeeper mathematics courses to African American, female, and low-socioeconomic students, and students with certain school assignments (Bowles & Gintis, 1976; Oakes, 1990a). Critics contend that race, gender, socioeconomic status, and the school assignment of students are significantly related to the enrollment recommendations students receive for mathematics courses during the scheduling process with guidance counselors. Critics of meritocracy suggest that factors such as race, gender, socioeconomic status, and school assignment are not extraneous from but rather are central to the measurement of academic ability. From this point of view, the gatekeeping process denies equitable educational opportunities for students who lack social privilege and therein denies them access to four-year institutions of higher education.

McClelland (1990) argued that students having "similar experiences will not respond to them in the same way . . ."

(p. 104). Students without social privilege are more likely to accept lower aspirations than their socially privileged counterparts. In addition to the biases existing in measures of academic ability, students without social privilege are less likely to have the determination necessary to seek and retain placement in the college preparatory track.

Statement of the Problem

The process of curriculum selection in the secondary school often finds equity, competence, and individual choice in conflict. Access to ninth-grade mathematics courses that are considered the gatekeepers to higher education, i.e., Algebra I or Geometry, is indicative of the conflicting factors in curriculum selection. If curriculum selection is based upon meritocratic principles, then academic ability as measured by standardized test scores will determine who will be given access to the college preparatory mathematics track regardless of race, gender, socioeconomic status, or school assignment. The question remains whether secondary schools do in fact adhere to the principles of meritocracy. If race, gender, socioeconomic status, or school assignment is a significant predictor of who will be denied access to college track mathematics courses, then the curriculum selection process is not meritocratic and access to the range of curriculum offerings is unfairly denied to students from certain segments of society.

Purpose of the Study

The purpose of this study was to measure the assignment of college track mathematics courses against a meritocratic definition of fairness to determine if access to certain college preparatory mathematics courses was denied to students from certain segments of society. More specifically, this study determined if race, gender, socioeconomic status, or school assignment taken independently as well as in combination were significant factors in predicting which students were assigned to the college preparatory mathematics track and which students were denied access to the college preparatory track. While controlling for academic ability, this study compared two groups of students--those who have been and those who have not been given access to Algebra I or Geometry, the gatekeeper mathematics courses.

Specifically, the research questions studied were as follows:

1. Were eighth-grade students who scored in the upper quartile in mathematics on a standardized achievement test scheduled into ninth-grade gatekeeper mathematics courses without regard to race?

2. Were eighth-grade students who scored in the upper quartile in mathematics on a standardized achievement test scheduled into ninth-grade gatekeeper mathematics courses without regard to gender?

3. Were eighth-grade students who scored in the upper quartile in mathematics on a standardized achievement test scheduled into ninth-grade gatekeeper mathematics courses without regard to socioeconomic status?

4. Were eighth-grade students who scored in the upper quartile in mathematics on a standardized achievement test scheduled into ninth-grade gatekeeper mathematics courses without regard to school assignment?

5. Were eighth-grade students who scored in the upper quartile in mathematics on a standardized achievement test scheduled into ninth-grade gatekeeper mathematics courses without regard to any combination of race, gender, socioeconomic status, or school assignment?

The 1992-1993 standardized Comprehensive Test of Basic Skills (CTBS) was used to control for academic ability and was accepted as valid and reliable for the purposes of this study. The CTBS, given throughout the United States to evaluate the academic progress of students in grades 2 through 10, was the only uniform measure of academic ability available for this study's population sample of 1993-1994 ninth-grade students. Academic ability was controlled during this study to eliminate the argument that certain students were denied gatekeeper mathematics courses because these students had lower measured academic abilities at the outset. If race, gender, socioeconomic status, or school assignment (either independently or in combination) was to be eliminated as a significant predictor of who was denied or admitted to gatekeeper mathematics courses, then the students in the sample should have a high level of measured academic ability at the outset.

This study dichotomized students into those who had been and those who had not been denied access to college track mathematics and then tested for four variables to determine if race, gender, socioeconomic status, and school assignment each were predictors of students' access to college preparatory mathematics curricula and if any combination of these variables was a significant predictor of students being denied access to college preparatory mathematics. To the extent that one or more of these variables or combination of variables were significant, the findings of this study would support the possibility that the curriculum scheduling process for mathematics college preparatory courses denied access to gatekeeper courses as measured against meritocracy's own definition of fairness. To the extent that one or more of these variables or combinations of variables were not significant, this study's findings would not support the contention that the curriculum scheduling process for college preparatory mathematics courses denied such access.

<u>Limitations</u>

This study had three major limitations:

1. The scope of the study was limited to a sampling of 1993-1994 ninth-grade students from one urban school district.

2. Academic ability was narrowly defined in this study in terms of a total mathematics score, mathematics computation score, or mathematics concepts and applications score on the standardized test, the Comprehensive Test of Basic Skills. Other factors that defined and influenced academic ability (e.g., motivation) were not considered.

3. Counselors assigned students to 1993-1994 ninth-grade mathematics courses based on objective measures of students' academic ability. Assignments made in accordance with meritocratic principles but subsequently refused or changed were not considered in this study because the information was not available. Examples of assignments made but not adhered to would include the following: students who were assigned to but refused enrollment in a gatekeeper mathematics course; parents who requested a lower level mathematics course in place of the assigned gatekeeper mathematics course; or students who entered a gatekeeper mathematics course, experienced difficulty and, at their own or their teacher's request, dropped to a lower level mathematics course.

Justification of the Study

Equity requires that even if unequal results are allowable under certain conditions, all students have a right to equal access to effective educational resources (Strike, 1982). The American public school system guarantees an open society in which students have a free and equal opportunity to achieve success. This study examined mathematics curriculum tracking which is one aspect of the critical role of the public school in making higher education accessible to all students regardless of race, socioeconomic status, gender, or school assignment.

Secondly, this study furthers an understanding of the process whereby a student is admitted to the college preparatory track and whether or not this process adheres to the principles of a meritocracy. While controlling for academic ability, this study examined socioeconomic status, race, gender, and school placement independently and in combination to determine if these variables were significant predictors of students being denied access to mathematics curriculum opportunities.

Definition of Terms

For the purposes of this study, the following terms were defined:

Academic ability was defined in terms of a total mathematics score, mathematics computation score, or mathematics concepts and applications score on the Comprehensive Test of Basic Skills (CTBS).

Egalitarian was used to describe the advocate who asserts the equality of all men.

Gatekeeper courses were defined as ninth-grade Algebra I or Geometry.

Gatekeeping process was defined as the curriculum scheduling by guidance counselors that either allows or prevents students from accessing college track mathematics courses.

Low-socioeconomic status was used to describe the economic standing of a student who qualified for free or reduced lunch during their eighth-grade year.

Meritocracy was used to describe the social philosophy based on rewarding individual achievement without regard to circumstances of birth.

Race was limited to the categories of African American, white, Hispanic, Asian, and native American.

School assignment was the school in which a student was enrolled on the last day of the ninth-grade year.

Social privilege was the result of a combination of socioeconomic status, race, gender, and school assignment.

Socioeconomic status (SES) was defined in terms of students' lunch payment status (free lunch, reduced lunch, or full payment lunch) at the end of their eighth-grade year.

CHAPTER 2

REVIEW OF RELATED LITERATURE

The history of the United States evidences a commitment to building an educated citizenry, and its emphasis on education has increased the proportion of the population who participate in secondary and postsecondary schooling. A meritocracy proposes equal access to a free education for all and stresses education as providing the gateway to greater social and economic opportunity. Course enrollment continues to account for differences in access to higher education. Access to critical high school curriculum programs, especially in mathematics, accounts for differentiation of opportunity and access to a college education. As long as access is based on individual merit and is not related to factors extraneous to individual ability, a meritocracy exists.

This study measured the assignment of college track mathematics courses against a meritocratic definition of fairness to determine if access to specific college preparatory mathematics courses was denied to students based on race, gender, socioeconomic status, and/or school assignment. Issues related to this study are presented in this review of the literature: meritocracy and its role in American society (specifically its role in education), the guidance counselor's role in a meritocracy, and student

access to gatekeeper mathematics courses, i.e., those
mathematics courses that allow students to seek entrance
into four-year colleges or universities.

<u>Meritocracy and The American Society</u>

Meritocracy has been given a central role in American
social philosophy. As an ideal, meritocracy means an equal
chance for people to compete and rise as far as their
abilities, drive, and determination will take them.

> A meritocratic system is based on achievement rather
> than ascription. In a meritocracy, awards,
> recognition, and the apportionment of goods and
> services would be based on demonstrated ability rather
> than seniority, race, religion, sex, nationality, and
> other artificial distinctions that are used to mete out
> the perquisites of life. (Rich & DeVitis, 1992, pp.
> 102-103)

The American meritocracy values achievement based on
ambition and striving. Paramount to a meritocracy is the
rewarding of an individual's efforts based on achievement,
without regard to such factors as circumstances of birth,
religious beliefs, ethnicity, gender, or economic status.

> The values of ambition and success would be impossible
> in a world where people do not believe they are
> rewarded on the basis of merit. If the values of
> ambition and success are to take hold, there must be a
> deep faith that one's status is not fixed, that
> opportunity is not limited, and that success is not
> accidental. Americans possess this faith in great
> measure. . . . (Webb & Sherman, 1989, p. 70)

The triumph of meritocracy in America is evidenced in
what is referred to as the national upper-middle-class
style: cosmopolitan and moderate (Jencks et al., 1972). A
meritocratic system advocates the elimination of unfair
competition in the form of unequal starts, but it justifies

unequal results on the basis of individual achievement
arising from natural abilities and talents (Bell, 1973).

The elements of a meritocratic society are succinctly
summarized by Webb and Sherman (1989):

> The ideal of equal opportunity implies an open rather
> than closed society. In a closed society, privilege
> (access to goods and services), power (the ability to
> get one's way despite resistance), and prestige (status
> and respect) are determined by birth and reinforced by
> custom and law. There is little mobility (movement up
> or down the stratification ladder), because social
> position is determined at birth. In a perfectly open
> society, access to material goods and services, which
> means access to money, would be determined solely by
> individual achievement. That is to say, in a perfectly
> open society all privilege is purchasable and access to
> money is determined solely by merit. Such a society is
> called meritocratic because privilege, prestige, and
> power are products of individual merit (ability and
> effort) rather than inherited privilege. (p. 490)

Meritocrats, who believe that individuals should enjoy
whatever status they are capable of achieving through their
own efforts, use rags to riches stories to emphasize their
position. Individual achievement, to the meritocrat, is
treasured and is a value never to be relinquished.
Frederick Jackson Turner (1903) wrote, "Western democracy
through the whole of its earlier period tended to the
production of a society of which the most distinctive fact
was the freedom of the individual to rise under conditions
of social mobility" (p. 83). Meritocrats maintain that
America has moved farther than any other nation in
emphasizing individual performance and cultivating vigor in
her citizens.

> Societies of hereditary privilege kept a lid on the
> aspirations of most individuals. With the lid removed,

aspirations soared. Men dared to hope, and they dared act in pursuit of their hopes. And constantly reinforcing their hope was the drama idden gifts discovered." Few themes have gripped the imagination of America so intensely as the discovery of talent in unexpected places--the slum child who shows scientific genius, the frail youngster who develops athletic skills, the poor boy who becomes a captain of industry. Our popular literature and our folklore are full of such images. They encourage self-discovery, stir ambition and inspire emulation. The American who wins success overnight traditionally insists, "I never dreamed it could happen to me!" But as surely as he is an American, that is precisely what he did dream. (Gardner, 1961, p. 17)

Meritocracy and Education

The American free public school system is a mechanism that should quarantee an open society in which children from all segments of society and from all social classes have an equal chance to develop their talents and achieve success. Education is closely tied to occupational placement and social mobility. If schools reward achievement rather than circumstances of birth, then the educational system is meritocratic. Education is the sorting agency in a meritocratic society, offering the most capable, high-achieving students higher education and then higher-paying jobs. Less capable students go as far as their abilities will take them in school and then on to more modest employment (Webb & Sherman, 1989).

A meritocratic society offers equal access to education, allowing students to develop the potentials most important to that society and achieve the rewards of employing those potentials. The sorting process in schools is accomplished through grading, tracking into specific courses, honors, and awards. "Those who fail will be notified that they were given a fair chance and must now assume societal roles consonant with demonstrated abilities" (Rich & DeVitis, 1992, p. 104).

A meritocratic society strives for equality of educational opportunity across all segments of society-- male and female, African American and white, rich and poor. The assumption is that access should not be related to characteristics that in principle are irrelevant to education, such as race, gender, socioeconomic standing, or school assignment (Rehberg & Rosenthal, 1978). For a meritocrat, this approach accepts the validity of native ability and acknowledges efforts toward influencing outcomes. Thus educational results may vary according to certain characteristics deemed "morally relevant" to the educational process but not according to "morally irrelevant" ones (Strike, 1982). A notion of equity requires that even if unequal results are allowable under certain conditions, all students have a right to equal access to effective educational resources. "Thus, the conception of equity . . . has two components, . . . equality of results across population subgroups, and . . . equality of access" (Gamoran, 1990, p. 157).

Egalitarianism and Education

Egalitarians, like meritocrats, share a fervor for equalizing opportunities for all people. Egalitarians, however, began to separate themselves from meritocrats because of "the perceived failures of government efforts to change the social order through an equalization of educational opportunity" (Webb & Sherman, 1989, p. 505).

Egalitarians would argue that, from a fully democratic perspective, a meritocracy should mean not only inclusion in the system but also the provision of appropriate conditions for learning. According to egalitarians, two tests of a meritocracy--equity across all segments and subgroups of society and equality of access to effective educational resources--have met with failure in America (Gamoran, 1990).

Egalitarians argue that determination and ability do not bridge the gap between unequal resources and high achievement.

> Where students do not display merit, where they do not meet the standards applied evenly to all, it may be concluded that failure is a matter of individual choice or deficiency. What we have arrived at is another incentive--and--punishment system, guided by the invisible hand of competition. (Bastian, Fruchter, Gittell, Greers, & Haskins, 1986, p. 22)

The "same chance" idea advocated by meritocrats means only that all children are granted access to school enrollment. The uneven distribution of materials and human resources is not acknowledged as contributors to unequal outcomes in achievement (Kozol, 1991). The meritocratic principle that commitment to equality can be achieved by offering each child the same structures of opportunity does not acknowledge the fact that children of different social classes and races are rarely provided with the same level of expenditure per pupil (Bastian et al., 1986). Rather than the "crisis of inequitable resourses, when a child fails--or simply fails to do well--this lack of achievement can be attributed to personal . . . deficiencies" (Bastian et al., 1986, p. 29). The meritocrat believes that entering the educational arena constitutes opportunity, and "the persistence of gross differentials in achievement is then made a question of personal merit" (Bastian et al., 1986, p. 29).

Children from different segments of society, social classes, and races enter school with varying degrees of advantages and disadvantages. Bastian et al. (1986) wrote that meritocrats disregard an important reason for school failure, that "children enter the schools with very unequal societal conditions influencing their performance" (p. 28).

Egalitarians are concerned that learning opportunities are stratified and, therefore, contribute to the reproduction of a stratified social order by offering greater opportunities to students from certain segments of society (George, 1988; Rosenbaum, 1987; Slavin, 1987, 1988). Opportunities are stratified within schools and between schools. Schools whose students are predominately white, middle-class, and relatively high achieving offer more chances for enriched and rigorous academic experiences (Gamoran, 1986; Oakes, 1990a, 1990b). Within school, stratifiers are also in place. Despite tests of academic ability, which meritocrats advocate as the fair way to determine the allocation of educational offerings, minority and lower socioeconomic students are less likely to be placed in college preparatory or high-ability courses (George, 1988; Lee & Ekstrom, 1987).

School Counselors, Academic Advising, and Meritocracy

One facet of the organizational process within the public school system that contributes to the furthering or hindrance of a meritocracy is guidance counseling. Guidance counseling for the middle school counselor encompasses many roles, one of the most important of which is that of academic advisor. The task of academic advising in middle schools is an effective way to bring personal meaning to the school experience. Academic advising includes helping students understand the middle school and high school curriculum sequences and how curriculum choices impact on future options. This academic advisement process utilizes the judgment of guidance counselors and to some degree the recommendations of teachers to determine a student's access to various courses and curriculum tracks. The middle school counselor must monitor each student's curriculum path and make certain that students are challenged in their curriculum schedule as needed.

The case for a strong academic advising program for middle school students has been heightened by the changing society. Mendel and Lincoln (1991) described the complexities of guidance needs of middle school students in the 1990s with a historical look at the job market:

In 1967, 41.1 percent of all jobs in America were held by high school dropouts, while college graduates held just 13.2 percent of all jobs. In 1987, dropouts held only 14.9 percent of the jobs; college graduates held 25.3 percent. Between now and the year 2000, the average new job will require two years of postsecondary education. Gone are the good old days. (p. 11)

Timely information about curriculum offerings and the consequences of choices is an important aspect of the middle school counselor's role as academic advisor. James Fenwick (1987), in a report to the California State Department of Education, espoused the virtues of ensuring that middle school students have access to critical information about the school curriculum:

Every middle grade student should have timely information about the relationship between the curricula of the middle and secondary grades and should be provided access to the opportunity to prepare for the broadest possible range of academic options, curriculum paths, in high school. (p. 61)

This academic counseling should be accomplished through a planned procedure in which the "logic and interrelatedness of the curriculum must be made clear" (Fenwick, 1987, p. 61). This planned procedure should be carried out by the middle school counselor, who has a thorough grasp of the relationship between the middle grade courses and the high school curriculum. A strong academic counseling program depends on clear communication of "the consequences of academic choices to students and the widening or narrowing of future options and opportunities based on personal educational decisions made in the middle grades" (Fenwick, 1987, p. 61).

When students understand their choices and the full
weight and meaning of those choices, this can be a basis for
a strong desire to stretch and strive to achieve
academically. Students decide on their high school
curriculum in the spring of their eighth-grade year.
"Students who receive academic counseling throughout the
middle grades can approach this important juncture in their
education with confidence when they know they are well
prepared for their transition to high school" (Fenwick,
1987, p. 62).

A crucial step in the academic advising process is the
placement of students in curriculum offerings (scheduling).
Guidance counselors, and to a lesser degree teachers,
control students' access to curriculum offerings through
this curriculum scheduling process (Lee & Ekstrom, 1987).
Typically, and according to meritocratic principles,
students are scheduled based upon the guidance counselor's
interpretations of and judgments about objective measures of
a student's academic abilities. For example, students who
score in the upper quartile on mathematics subtests of a
standardized measurement of academic ability are placed in
college track mathematics courses. This scheduling process
establishes guidance counselors as the critical gatekeepers
in a student's progress through the educational pipeline
(Commission on Precollege Guidance and Counseling, 1986).

Additionally, the middle school counselor must monitor
students' progress in their assigned or chosen curriculum

paths. "Student options must be paralleled by a monitoring of their achievement. Care must be taken to make certain that remedial, regular, or accelerated instruction pushes all students toward their maximum levels of individual ability" (Fenwick, 1987, p. 62). Students, therefore, must also develop a clear understanding of their identities and competencies.

> It is at this point [middle school] that many students form lifelong values and attitudes about the significance of education and their own chances of succeeding in upwardly mobile academic and career choices. It is for these reasons that students need to grasp conceptually the potential of their own lives. They must receive the affirmation and motivation which will cause them to strive to attain their highest and best scholastic efforts. Academic counseling is a powerful factor in this process. (Fenwick, 1987, pp. 62-63)

Academic Advising: Race, Socioeconomic Status, Gender, and School Assignment.

Accurate information upon which to base academic plans and personal decisions about their future is a basic right of all middle school students. A meritocracy requires an equal chance for people to compete. Mendel & Lincoln (1991) voiced concerns that academic counseling efforts do not place all children on equal footing.

> Only a lucky handful of our children are supported, encouraged, and challenged sufficiently to reach their full potential as students and as people. . . . They wake up in their caps and gowns the morning after graduation, their heads pounding with a hangover (literal or figurative, perhaps both) and they wonder, often for the first time: What now? (p. vii)

Students make decisions that are inconsistent with their future goals, both with or without academic advising assistance (Litten, 1982). In 1986, the College Entrance Examination Board found that by the tenth grade only half of ninth-graders who said they were going to college were enrolled in courses that would qualify them for college entrance (Commission on Precollege Guidance and Counseling, 1986).

Discrepancies for members of certain segments of society continue to exist in postsecondary education attainment. Egalitarians are concerned that this may be evidence of uneven academic advisement efforts in secondary schools (Lee & Ekstrom, 1987). The current status of minority enrollment in higher education reveals a complex pattern of gains and slowdowns.

> Hispanics and women continue to increase their share of the total enrollment but blacks experience a slackening momentum. . . . Minority groups, especially blacks and Hispanics, suffer from inadequate secondary school preparation and counseling and from economic and psychometric barriers. They are disproportionly overrepresented in two-year institutions and underrepresented in four-year colleges and graduate and professional schools. (Preer, 1981, p. 1)

Pelavin and Kane (1990) reported the total enrollment in institutions of higher education by race/ethnicity from 1976 to 1986. Their findings revealed both increases and losses. All groups increased their enrollment during this period; African American students increased by 5 percent, Hispanics by more than 60 percent, white students by 9 percent, and Asian students by 125 percent. The enrollment for African American students was reported as remaining significantly below the rate for white students.

Equity is a vital consideration in a strong, meritocratic, comprehensive, academic counseling program. Every student must be involved in the counseling process without regard to race, religion, nationality, gender, school assignment, or any other artificial distinction, in order for the process to be meritocratic (Lee & Ekstrom, 1987).

Gatekeeper Mathematics Courses and Meritocracy

A meritocracy demands that students with proven academic abilities be given access to the curriculum choices that afford the greatest opportunities, the college preparatory track. Geometry and Algebra I are the curriculum choices that open the gates to postsecondary education and, therefore, most differentiate opportunities for students (Oakes, 1990a).

Through the analysis of nearly 16,000 American young people, Pelavin and Kane (1990) demonstrated the critical role that Geometry and Algebra I have on college attendance and completion rates. "Virtually all students who plan to attend college and take Geometry [emphasis mine] in high school go to college regardless of their race or ethnicity" (p. viii). Pelavin and Kane (1990) also found that courses that improve the odds that collegiate success will follow are courses that students take early in their high school careers, such as Algebra I and Geometry.

> While 58 percent of white students attended some college within four years of graduation from high school, only 47 percent of black and 45 percent of

Hispanic students did so. That is, minorities attended college at only 70 percent of the rate of white students. Poor students attended college at only 61 percent of the rate of attendance of non-poor students. However, among students who had completed a course in high school geometry, 80 percent of black students in this group attended college along with 82 percent of Hispanic students and 83 percent of white students. The gap between minorities and whites virtually disappears among students who took geometry. Among poor students who took geometry the gap was diminished by half, although it was not eliminated. (p. viii)

Taking Geometry was associated with a reduced gap between the college attendance rates of African American and whites and Hispanics and whites. The base rates of college attendance showed that the African American-to-white ratio of students attending any college within four years of high school graduation is 80 percent, and the Hispanic-to-white ratio is 76 percent. Among students taking Geometry, these ratios are 96 percent and 99 percent, respectively (Pelavin & Kane, 1990).

A similar reduction is apparent in the gap between students from the lowest and highest income groups when Geometry is taken into account. Seventy-one percent of the students in the lowest income group who take Geometry attend some college within four years of high school, while only 36 percent of those who do not take Geometry do so (Pelavin & Kane, 1990). Two striking facts emerge from Pelavin and Kane's (1990) analysis: "A vast majority of the students who take Geometry go to college. This finding is true regardless of race or income" (p. 50).

Summary

The American public school system is the mechanism by which all children are given the opportunity to develop their potentials and achieve the rewards of employing those potentials. A meritocratic educational system recognizes the validity of native ability and acknowledges that educational results and opportunities may vary according to ability but must be unrelated to characteristics that are irrelevant to education.

The assignment of educational opportunities is primarily accomplished by school counselors and other educators through the assignment of curriculum pathways based on objective measures of an individual's academic ability. A meritocracy demands that students with proven academic abilities be given access to the curriculum pathways that offer the greatest opportunities, the college preparatory track. For a ninth-grade student, Algebra I or geometry are the gatekeeper courses to the college preparatory track. Denial or admission to these gatekeeper mathematics courses most differentiate opportunities for students beyond high school. Egalitarians are concerned that the assignment of gatekeeper mathematics courses based on objective measures contributes to the reproduction of the social order because objective measures favor students of social privilege. Additionally, the egalitarians maintain that despite tests of academic ability, minority and lower socioeconomic students are less likely to be placed in college preparatory mathematics.

CHAPTER 3

RESEARCH METHODOLOGY

This study measured the gatekeeping process against a meritocratic definition of fairness to determine if this process denied access to the college preparatory mathematics courses to students from particular segments of society. This chapter includes a discussion of the methodology that was employed, the study's null hypothesis, and statistical applications.

Research Questions and Null Hypotheses

Research questions were posed to investigate the curriculum selection process for gatekeeper mathematics courses against a meritocratic definition of fairness to determine if this process denied admission to the college preparatory mathematics track to students from particular segments of society when the variable of academic ability was controlled. The following questions were posed:

1. Were eighth-grade students who scored in the upper quartile in mathematics on a standardized achievement test scheduled into ninth-grade gatekeeper mathematics courses without regard to race?

2. Were eighth-grade students who scored in the upper quartile in mathematics on a standardized achievement test scheduled into ninth-grade gatekeeper mathematics courses

without regard to gender?

3. Were eighth-grade students who scored in the upper quartile in mathematics on a standardized achievement test scheduled into ninth-grade gatekeeper mathematics courses without regard to socioeconomic status?

4. Were eighth-grade students who scored in the upper quartile in mathematics on a standardized achievement test scheduled into ninth-grade gatekeeper mathematics courses without regard to school assignment?

5. Were eighth-grade students who scored in the upper quartile in mathematics on a standardized achievement test scheduled into ninth-grade gatekeeper mathematics courses without regard to any combination of race, gender, socioeconomic status, or school assignment?

The following null hypotheses were tested:

Ho_1: Race was not statistically significant in determining who had been denied admission to gatekeeper mathematics courses when academic ability was controlled.

Ho_2: Gender was not statistically significant in determining who had been denied admission to gatekeeper mathematics courses when academic ability was controlled.

Ho_3: Socioeconomic status was not statistically significant in determining who had been denied admission to gatekeeper mathematics courses when academic ability was controlled.

Ho_4: School assignment was not statistically significant in determining who had been denied admission to gatekeeper mathematics courses when academic ability was controlled.

Ho_5: Any combination of race, gender, socioeconomic status, and/or school assignment was not statistically significant in determining who had been denied admission to gatekeeper mathematics courses when academic ability was controlled.

Definition of Variables

Race, one of the four predictor variables, was defined using five categories: white, African American, Asian, Hispanic, and Native American. These five categories were used because the school system from which this study's sample was drawn organized its student information database into these five ethnic groups.

Socioeconomic status was defined by a student's lunch paying status, i.e., free lunch, reduced lunch, or fully-paid lunch. For the purpose of this study, students on free or reduced lunch for the 1992-1993 school year were defined as low-socioeconomic students. The 1992-1993, eighth-grade, lunch-paying status for these students was used instead of the 1993-1994 ninth-grade year because the middle school lunch-paying patterns were better indicators of a student's financial situation. A large percentage of these students upon entering high school discontinued applying for free or reduced lunch even though their economic status had not changed. During the 1993-1994 school year, the sample school system had 37 percent fewer ninth-grade students applying for free or reduced lunch than had applied as eighth-grade students during the 1992-1993 school year. The income level and household size that qualified a student for free or reduced lunch during the 1992-1993 school year is presented in Table 1. Household size in Table 1 was defined as all persons in a household excluding only those persons who may be boarders or renters. For example, if two friends and their children lived together and shared expenses, all were considered in the total household size. Income was defined as gross wages from all members of the household, including the wages of minors.

School assignment was determined by one of sixteen high schools to which a student was assigned on the last day of ninth grade for the 1993-1994 school year. Sixeen of the seventeen high schools in the school system from which the sample was drawn were included. The omitted high school was a college preparatory magnet school in which only college preparatory mathematics courses were available.

Academic ability was a moderator variable at the time of eighth-grade scheduling. For the purpose of this study, academic ability was defined as students' mathematical computation score, mathematical concepts and applications score, or total mathematics score on the eighth-grade CTBS test. The sample included all students who scored in the upper quartile on any one of these three mathematics

Table 1

Income Eligibility Guidelines for Free And Reduced Price Meals

Effective from July 1, 1992 to June 30, 1993

Guidelines for Free Meals	
Household Size	Gross Yearly Income in Dollars
2	11,947
3	15,041
4	18,135
5	21,229
6	24,323
7	27,417
8	30,511
Guidelines for Reduced Price Meals	
Household Size	Gross Yearly Income in Dollars
2	17,002
3	21,405
4	25,808
5	30,211
6	34,614
7	39,017
8	43,420

Source: Department of Education for this state, 1993

subtests. The academic ability variable was included in order to control for discrepancies in student academic ability at the time of course scheduling for high school.

Mathematics course placement was the dichotomous criterion variable used to evaluate the gatekeeper process. Gatekeeper mathematics courses had been denied for any eighth-grade students who had been scheduled for any of the following ninth-grade mathematics courses: Exploratory Mathematics I, Exploratory Mathematics II, Consumer Mathematics, Applied Mathematics I, Applied Mathematics II, Liberal Arts Mathematics, Integrated Mathematics, or Pre-Algebra. On the other hand, ninth-grade students enrolled in Algebra I, Geometry, Geometry Honors, Algebra II or Algebra II Honors had not been denied access to gatekeeper mathematics courses.

Only a small percentage of students take Algebra II as ninth-grade students; for the school year 1994-1995, 78 or .009 percent of the ninth-grade students in the school system in this study were enrolled in Algebra II. Therefore, Algebra I and Geometry were considered gatekeeper mathematics courses, whereas Algebra II in ninth grade was not included because it is very rarely offered and is intended for only the most advanced students (Oakes, 1990a).

Design of the Study

This study employed a multiple correlational design (multiple regression) with a dichotomous rather than a continuous criterion variable, i.e., having been denied access to gatekeeper mathematics courses or not having been denied access to gatekeeper mathematics courses. The criterion variable originated from the understanding that the college preparatory mathematics track required a minimum of Algebra I or Geometry in ninth grade. This study involved correlating four predictor variables with a single dichotomous criterion variable; therefore, a special application called "logistic regression" was employed to describe the association between variables. Logistic regression was used to determine if a relationship existed singly or in combination between the four predictor variables of race, gender, socioeconomic status, or school assignment and the criterion variable of having been denied access to gatekeeper mathematics courses or not having been denied access to gatekeeper mathematics courses.

Egalitarians have argued that academic ability as measured by standardized tests is related to the race, gender, SES, and/or school assignment of students. As a result, the relationships between the moderator variable of academic ability and the four predictor variables were examined independently and in combination.

As modeled by logistic regression, the association that existed between each predictor variable and the criterion variable, singly and in combination, was reported. An analysis of how well the linear association described the data was examined by a "goodness-of-fit" model (Brase & Brase, 1991). Terms of probability described the likelihood of each of the four predictor variables (race, gender, SES, and school assignment) becoming a determinant of the criterion variable.

Population and Sampling Procedures

This study examined 7745 academic records of all enrolled 1993-1994 ninth-grade students from 16 high schools in a large, urban school system. The sample for this study was chosen by identifying all students who fell in the upper quartile on the 1992-1993, eighth-grade CTBS test in either mathematics computation, mathematics concepts and applications, and/or total mathematics. Of the 7745 records examined, 1611 students scored in the upper quartile on a mathematics subtest. Gender, race, socioeconomic status, school assignment, CTBS mathematics results, and 1993-1994 school assignment also were available for the 1611 students selected for the sample. The ethnic and gender breakdown for this study's sample is presented in Table 2.

Setting of the Study

The study population was drawn from a large, urban school district with a student population of more than 120,000 (the district ranks in the top 15 in the nation in size). The school system was selected for study because it was typical of the other school systems of the state in that students in secondary schools were tracked according to professed meritocratic principles into college preparatory mathematics courses, general mathematics courses, or

Table 2

Frequency and Percent of Race and Gender of Sample

Characteristic	Frequency	Percent
Race		
African American	242	15.02
Asian	88	5.46
Hispanic	32	1.99
Native American	4	.25
White	1245	77.28
Gender		
Female	835	51.83
Male	776	48.17
Race by Gender		
African American Female	126	7.82
African American Male	116	7.20
Asian Female	43	2.67
Asian Male	45	2.79
Hispanic Female	13	0.81
Hispanic Male	19	1.18
Native American Female	2	0.12
Native American Male	2	0.12
White Female	651	40.42
White Male	594	36.87

Source: Student Information Management System for this
School System, 1994

vocational courses; the scheduling of students in gatekeeper mathematics courses was conducted by school counselors in the manner typically found in this state's secondary schools; at 56 percent white and 44 percent minority, this school system closely paralleled the total count for this state's schools in majority/minority breakdown (59 percent white and 41 percent minority); the school systems' gender population of 49 percent females and 51 percent males was the same as the gender count for the schools of this state; and student demographic, standardized testing, financial, and course placement data existed and were accessible.

An examination of the 1993-1994 mathematics tracking patterns for the students in this school system revealed that: 52.55 percent of high school students were enrolled in Algebra I or above; 34 percent of this school's 7745 ninth-grade students were enrolled in a gatekeeper mathematics course (Algebra I or Geometry); of the 5020 graduating seniors, 61 percent had completed at least one college track mathematics course before graduating, and of this group, 56 percent had successfully completed Geometry (Student Information Management System for this School System, 1995).

The scheduling procedures for this school system's 1992-1993 eighth-grade students were basically the same in all 25 middle schools and were typical of the scheduling procedures found in secondary schools across the nation (Lee & Ekstrom, 1987). High school course scheduling for eighth-grade students began in the spring of the eighth-grade year and started with large group presentations and then moved to individual counseling sessions.

Each middle school conducted a large group orientation program that included information on the curriculum sequence, the college preparatory courses, vocational training offerings, academic requirements for certain scholarships, and the procedures to be followed for course selection. This large group program was followed by individual advising sessions in which a counselor worked with each eighth-grade student in determining courses for each of the seven periods in a high school day. The counselor referred to certain information on each student to determine course placement, i.e., permanent record of all courses taken, current report card, cumulative standardized test record, and teacher recommendations. Students were scheduled using these four pieces of information with emphasis on the objective data--the cumulative test record. By adhering to an objective record of students' academic ability, the principles of a meritocracy should be in practice (Bastian et al., 1986). If a student wanted to take a higher-level course than was advised, the student was required to sign a course waiver. The course waiver explained the risk in taking a course beyond one's ability; if the course proves to be too difficult, the student may not be able to transfer to a lower level class because teachers are hired and courses are scheduled based on the course selections made in the spring.

Data Collection Procedures

The computerized, cumulative test record file for each 1993-1994 ninth-grade student in this school system was examined and the sample was selected by identifying all students who scored in the upper quartile on any one of three, 1992-1993, CTBS mathematics subtests. The computerized data files were searched to identify each student's identification number, race, gender, 1993-1994 school assignment, lunch-paying status for the 1992-1993 school year, course number for 1993-1994 mathematics assignment, and the percentile on each of three, 1992-1993, CTBS mathematics subtests. These data then were used to test the claim that meritocratic criteria alone were significant in determining who had been denied access to the gatekeeper mathematics courses and who had not been denied access to the gatekeeper mathematics courses.

The data collection procedures were approved by the Director of Research and Evaluation for the school system in this study and by the Institutional Review Board at the University of Florida.

Statistical Procedures

A logistic regression was employed to test the null hypotheses. This linear model was used because the criterion variable, having been or not been denied gatekeeper mathematics courses, was dichotomous instead of continuous as in the case of most regression models (Agresti, 1990). The logistic regression statistic had the capability of determining the relationship between the criterion variable and multiple predictor variables (SES, race, gender, and school assignment) taken independently and in combination.

CHAPTER 4

RESULTS

This study measured the mathematics gatekeeping process
(Commission on Precollege Guidance and Counseling, 1986;
Oakes, 1990a) against a meritocratic definition of fairness
to determine if this process denied access to gatekeeper
courses to students of certain races, gender, socioeconomic
status or school assignment. The results of this study are
presented in this chapter. Included are descriptive
characteristics of the sample, the study's null hypotheses,
the relationships between various predictor and the
controlled variable, and a summary of the study's findings.

Descriptive Characteristics of the Sample

Analyses were run for 242 African American students, 88
Asian students, 32 Hispanic students, 4 Native American
students, and 1245 white students, for a total sample of
1611 students. Of these 1611 students, 433, or 27 percent,
were denied admission to the gatekeeper mathematics courses.
These 1611 students from the 1993-1994 ninth grade scored in
the upper quartile on one of three CTBS mathematics subtests
during their eighth-grade year. The 1992-1993 CTBS summary
report for these eighth-grade students showed the following
frequency for each mathematics subtest: 6379 students had a
mathematics computation score (200 students were missing

this information); 6376 students had a mathematics concepts and applications score (203 students were missing this information); and 6327 students had a total mathematics score (252 students were missing this information).

The socioeconomic status for each student was determined by accessing their 1992-1993 lunch paying status. Students eligible for free or reduced lunch were defined as low-socioeconomic. Six percent, or 103 students, fell into the low-socioeconomic category.

Table 2 (supra, p. 35) presents race and gender composition for the students in this study. Asian students at 5.46 percent of the sample and white students at 77.28 percent of the sample were represented in the sample in greater numbers than their frequency in the ninth-grade population from which the sample was drawn (2.6 and 55.9 respectively). African American students at 15.02 percent, Hispanic students at 1.99 percent, and Native American students at .25 percent were underrepresented in this sample in comparison to their numbers in the population (39.0, 2.4, and 1.0 respectively). The gender composition of the sample, 51.83 percent female and 48.17 percent male, was comparable to the gender composition of the population from which the sample was drawn, at 49.2 percent females and 50.8 percent males.

Research Questions and Null Hypotheses

Research questions were posed to investigate the curriculum selection process for gatekeeper mathematics courses against a meritocratic definition of fairness to determine if this process denied admission to the college preparatory mathematics track to students from particular segments of society when the variable of academic ability was controlled. The following questions were posed:

1. Were eighth-grade students who scored in the upper quartile in mathematics on a standardized achievement test scheduled into ninth-grade gatekeeper mathematics courses without regard to race?

2. Were eighth-grade students who scored in the upper quartile in mathematics on a standardized achievement test scheduled into ninth-grade gatekeeper mathematics courses without regard to gender?

3. Were eighth-grade students who scored in the upper quartile in mathematics on a standardized achievement test scheduled into ninth-grade gatekeeper mathematics courses without regard to socioeconomic status?

4. Were eighth-grade students who scored in the upper quartile in mathematics on a standardized achievement test scheduled into ninth-grade gatekeeper mathematics courses without regard to school assignment?

5. Were eighth-grade students who scored in the upper quartile in mathematics on a standardized achievement test scheduled into ninth-grade gatekeeper mathematics courses without regard to any combination of race, gender, socioeconomic status, or school assignment?

Analyses were run with the full logistic regression model, examining the main effects of all predictor variables with the criterion variable as well as interactions between all of these variables. Predictor variables included race, gender, socioeconomic status, and school assignment. The criterion variable was gatekeeper mathematics course placement.

The interpretation of these results revealed some significant relationships with the criterion variable. In this study, school assignment, socioeconomic status, and the combination of gender and socioeconomic status were found to be significantly related to students' placement into gatekeeper mathematics. These significant contrasts are reported in Tables 3 through 5. Complete frequency and percent tables for these and all other main and interactive effects are reported in Appendix B. These significant relationships resulted in research questions 3, 4, and 5 being answered in the negative and in the rejection of the following three null hypotheses:

Ho_3: Socioeconomic status was not statistically significant in determining who had been denied admission to gatekeeper mathematics courses when academic ability was controlled.

Ho_4: School assignment was not statistically significant in determining who had been denied admission to gatekeeper mathematics courses when academic ability was controlled.

Ho_5: Any combination of race, gender, socioeconomic status, and/or school assignment was not statistically significant in determining who had been denied admission to gatekeeper mathematics courses when academic ability was controlled.

The statistically significant relationship between socioeconomic status and gatekeeper mathematics course placement (Table 3) meant that the investigation into the following research question resulted in a negative response: Were eighth-grade students who scored in the upper quartile in mathematics on a standardized achievement test scheduled into ninth-grade gatekeeper mathematics courses without regard to socioeconomic status? An odds ratio is a measurement of association that approximates how much more likely (or unlikely) it was for high-socioeconomic students to be admitted or denied admission into gatekeeper mathematics as compared to the reference group, low-socioeconomic students. An odds ratio >1.0 had a greater likelihood for admission to gatekeeper courses than the reference group. An odds ratio <1.0 means that there was

Table 3

Logistic Regression Analysis of Maximum Likelihood Estimates for Socioeconomic Status (SES) on Gatekeeper Mathematics Placement

Predictor		Wald Chi-Square	Pr> Chi-Square	Odds Ratio
SES	H vs L	6.29	.01*	3.21

Note: H = High-Socioeconomic Status; L = Low-Socioeconomic Status less likelihood for admission. Analysis revealed a strong association with high-socioeconomic students being three times more likely to be placed into gatekeeper mathematics courses than low-socioeconomic students (odds ratio = 3.2).

The statistically significant relationship between school assignment and gatekeeper mathematics course placement meant that the investigation into the following research question resulted in a negative response: Were eighth-grade students who scored in the upper quartile in mathematics on a standardized achievement test scheduled into ninth-grade gatekeeper mathemetics courses without regard to school assignment? Table 4 presents an analysis

Table 4

Logistic Regression Analysis of Maximum Likelihood Estimates for School Assignment on Gatekeeper Mathematics Placement

Predictor		Wald Chi-Square	Pr> Chi-Square	Odds Ratio
School[1]	2 vs 16	4.27	.04	2.64
	5 vs 16	10.50	.00	2.46
	7 vs 16	6.72	.01	5.09
	8 vs 16	8.94	.00	3.02
	10 vs 16	11.87	.00	2.69
	11 vs 16	15.11	.00	3.12
	13 vs 16	6.18	.01	2.17
	15 vs 16	10.84	.00	2.38

Note: [1] = only significant contrasts for this effect are shown.

of maximum likelihood estimates in which eight schools related significantly with admission into gatekeeper mathematics. The school with identifier number 16 was least likely to schedule students into gatekeeper mathematics and became the reference school for this study. Schools with identifier numbers 2, 5, 7, 8, 10, 11, 13, and 15 were significantly more likely than the reference school to schedule students into gatekeeper mathematics courses. School 8 (odds ratio = 3.02) and school 11 (odds ratio = 3.12) were three times more likely to schedule students into gatekeeper mathematics than reference school 16. School 7 was five times more likely to schedule students into gatekeeper mathematics than the reference school (odds ratio = 5.09. School 1 (odds ratio = 1.25), school 3 (odds ratio = 1.10), school 6 (odds ratio = 1.11), school 12 (odds ratio = 1.30) scheduled students into gatekeeper mathematics at only a slightly higher rate than the reference school.

Frequency and percent tables were established for analysis between the covariate (admission into gatekeeper mathematics courses) and the predictor variable of school assignment in combination with race, gender, and SES. An analysis of the interactions between these variables using the logistic regression procedure was hindered because of the small frequencies found in many of the cells. Maximum likelihood estimates could only be performed on the following three interactions: race and gender, socioeconomic status and race, and socioeconomic status and gender. Only one combination of these three interactions was significant: socioeconomic status and gender. Therefore, the investigation into research question 5 resulted in a negative response to the following question: Were eighth-grade students who scored in the upper quartile in mathematics on a standardized achievement test scheduled into ninth-grade mathematics courses without regard to the combination of socioeconomic status and gender?

A maximum likelihood analysis (Table 5) revealed that high-socioeconomic males were 77 percent (odds ratio = .23) less likely than the reference group, low-socioeconomic females, to be scheduled into gatekeeper mathematics courses once the effects of gender and socioeconomic status were taken into account. This significant relationship (p, .00) was an unexpected finding for this combination of gender and socioeconomic status because males were more likely to be scheduled into gatekeeper mathematics courses and

Table 5

Logistic Regression Analysis of Maximum Likelihood Estimates for Interactions of Gender and Socioeconomic Status on Gatekeeper Mathematics Placement

Predictor		Wald Chi-Square	Pr> Chi-Square	Odds Ratio
Gender	HM vs LF[1]	8.83	.00	.23

Note: [1] = No other interactions were significant. HM = High-Socioeconomic Status Males; LF = Low-Socioeconomic Status Females

high-socioeconomic students were more likely to be placed
into gatekeeper mathematics.

The logistic regression analysis was used to examine
the main effects of the predictor variable of race. This
effect was found to be unrelated to gatekeeper mathematics
course placement. Race was not statistically significant in
determining who had been denied admission to gatekeeper
mathematics courses when academic ability was controlled.
Therefore, the investigation into the following research
question yielded an affirmative response: Were eighth-grade
students who scored in the upper quartile in mathematics on
a standardized achievement test scheduled into ninth-grade
gatekeeper mathematics courses without regard to race? The
analysis of maximum likelihood estimates for race and
admission to gatekeeper mathematics (Table 6) did not yield
statistically significant relationships but did yield strong
associations.

Table 6

Logistic Regression Analysis of Maximum Likelihood Estimates
for Race on Gatekeeper Mathematics Placement

	Predictor	Wald Chi-Square	Pr> Chi-Square	Odds Ratio
Race	A vs W	2.74	.10	7.19
	AA vs W	.11	.74	.85
	H vs W	1.00	.32	3.93

Note: A = Asian; W = White; AA = African American;
H = Hispanic

The white race was used as the reference group against which Asians, African Americans, and Hispanics were compared. The maximum likelihood analysis for the Asian race revealed a strong association. The Asian race was seven times more likely to be placed into gatekeeper mathematics courses than the white race (odds ratio = 7.19). The Hispanic race was almost four times more likely to be placed into gatekeeper mathematics courses than the white race (odds ratio = 3.93), and the African American race was less likely to be placed into gatekeeper mathematics courses than the white race at 85 percent the rate of white students (odds ratio = .85). There were too few Native Americans (4) in the study for an analysis of maximum likelihood. Although the odds ratio showed a measure of association between the predictor variable of race and the criterion variable of gatekeeper mathematics, there were no statistically significant relationships between the criterion variable of gatekeeper mathematics and the three nonwhite races.

Gender was not statistically significant in determining who had been denied admission to gatekeeper mathematics courses when academic ability was controlled. A measure of association was found between gender and gatekeeper mathematics; however, the association was not statistically significant (.06 level). Therefore, the investigation into the following research question yielded an affirmative response: Were eighth-grade students who scored in the upper quartile in mathematics on a standardized achievement test scheduled into ninth-grade gatekeeper mathematics courses without regard to gender? The analysis of the maximum likelihood estimates, presented in Table 7, showed males to be two and one-half times more likely to be admitted to gatekeeper mathematics courses than females (odds ratio = 2.54).

Relationships between Predictor and Controlled Variables

Egalitarians have argued that academic ability as measured by standardized tests is directly tied to the race, gender, socioeconomic status, and school assignment of students. Therefore, an analysis of variance was applied to determine the relationship between these variables (Tables 8, 9, and 10). The academic ability covariate was defined as a score on any one of three CTBS subtests, that is, total mathematics, mathematics computation, and/or mathematics concepts and applications. Analyses were conducted between each of these three CTBS subtests and race, gender, socioeconomic status and school assignment independently and

Table 7

Logistic Regression Analysis of Maximum Likelihood Estimates for Gender on Gatekeeper Mathematics Placement

Predictor		Wald Chi-Square	Pr> Chi-Square	Odds Ratio
Gender	Male vs Female	3.58	.06	2.54

in combination to determine if a relationship existed.
Analyses revealed that academic ability and school
assignment were significantly related for all three
covariates (total mathematics $p<.00$, mathematics computation
$p<.02$, mathematics concepts and applications $p<.00$).
Academic ability, as measured by the total mathematics
score, was also found to be related to race ($p<.03$).
Additionally, analysis revealed that the combination of race
and socioeconomic status was significantly related to
academic ability as measured by the mathematics computation
score ($p<.03$).

Table 8

Analysis of Variance of Academic Ability (Total Mathematics)
and Main and Interaction Effects of Predictor Variables

Effect	DF	Sum of Squares	Mean Square	F Value	Pr > F
Race	4	2691.42	672.85	2.68	.03*
Gender	1	15.49	15.49	.06	.80
Race*Gender	4	129.89	32.47	.13	.97
SES	1	2.58	2.58	.01	.92
Race*SES	3	729.80	243.26	.97	.41
Gender*SES	1	352.93	352.93	1.40	.24
Race*Gender *SES	3	21.63	7.21	.03	.99
School	15	11989.15	799.28	3.18	.00*

Note: SES = Socioeconomic Status

In that egalitarians also anticipate that socioeconomic status is tied to the race, gender, and school assignment of students, the relationships between these predictor variables were examined (Table 11 through 13). A logistic regression analysis applied to socioeconomic status and race crosstabulation (Table 11) yielded a significant chi-square value of 61.45 (4 d.f., $p<.00$) for 10 cells. Therefore, any cell chi-square above 6.14 contributed to the significant relationship that was shown to exist between socioeconomic status and race. Thus, white students had significantly

Table 9

Analysis of Variance of Academic Ability (Mathematics Computation) and Main and Interaction Effects of Predictor Variables

Effect	DF	Sum of Squares	Mean Square	F Value	Pr > F
Race	4	1570.12	392.53	2.02	.09
Gender	1	63.28	63.28	.33	.57
Race*Gender	4	165.99	41.50	.21	.93
SES	1	136.54	136.54	.70	.40
Race*SES	3	1759.08	586.36	3.02	.03
Gender*SES	1	330.23	330.23	1.70	.19
Race*Gender *SES	3	48.24	16.08	.08	.97
School	15	5441.22	362.75	1.87	.02*

Note: SES = Socioeconomic Status

less representation in the low-socioeconomic category than would be expected (cell chi-square = 11.79), and African American students had significantly greater representation in the low-socioeconomic category than would be expected by chance (cell chi-square = 39.19).

Additionally, a significant relationship (chi-square = 61.14, with 15 d.f., p,<.00) was shown to exist between socioeconomic status and school assignment (Table 12). The overall chi-square value of 61.14 divided by 32 (i.e., the number of cells) determined the critical value of 1.91 for

Table 10

Analysis of Variance of Academic Ability (Mathematics Concepts and Applications) and Main and Interaction Effects of Predictor Variables

Effect	DF	Sum of Squares	Mean Square	F Value	Pr > F
Race	4	1297.27	324.32	1.98	.09
Gender	1	46.82	46.82	.29	.59
Race*Gender	4	54.42	13.61	.08	.99
SES	1	53.16	53.16	.32	.57
Race*SES	3	1053.03	351.01	2.14	.09
Gender*SES	1	367.60	367.60	2.24	.13
Race*Gender *SES	3	12.89	4.30	.03	.99
School	15	5536.64	369.11	2.25	.00*

Note: SES = Socioeconomic Status

Table 11

<u>Chi-Square Test Comparing Socioeconomic Status (SES) by</u>
<u>Race</u>

Frequency Expected Cell Chi-Square Percent Row Percent Column Percent	High SES	Low SES	Total
Asian	79 82.37 .14 4.91 89.77 5.24	9 5.63 2.02 .56 10.23 8.74	88 5.47
African American	201 225.58 2.68 12.48 83.40 13.34	40 15.42 39.19 2.48 16.60 38.83	241 14.97
Hispanic	27 29.95 .29 1.68 84.38 1.79	5 2.05 4.26 .31 15.63 4.85	32 1.99
Native American	4 3.74 .02 .25 100.00 .27	0 .26 .26 .00 .00 .00	4 .25
White	1196 1165.40 .81 74.29 96.06 79.36	49 79.65 11.79 3.04 3.94 47.57	1245 7.33
Total	1507 93.60	103 6.40	1610 100.00

Table 12

Chi-Square Test Comparing Socioeconomic Status (SES) by School

Frequency Expected Cell Chi-Square Percent Row Percent Column Percent	High SES	Low SES	Total
School #1	46 50.54 .41 2.86 85.19 3.05	8 3.45 5.98 .50 14.81 7.77	54 3.35
School #2	29 29.95 .03 1.80 90.63 1.92	3 2.05 .44 .19 9.38 2.91	32 1.99
School #3	10 12.17 .39 .62 76.92 .66	3 .83 5.65 .19 23.08 2.91	13 .81
School #4	11 12.17 .11 .68 84.62 .73	2 .83 1.64 .12 15.38 1.94	13 .81
School #5	173 175.97 .05 10.75 92.02 11.48	15 12.03 .73 .93 7.98 14.56	188 11.68

Table 12--continued

Frequency Expected Cell Chi-Square Percent Row Percent Column Percent	High SES	Low SES	Total
School #6	87 87.99 .01 5.40 92.55 5.77	7 6.01 .16 .43 7.45 6.80	94 5.84
School #7	17 18.72 .16 1.06 85.00 1.13	3 1.28 2.31 .19 15.00 2.91	20 1.24
School #8	71 68.33 .10 4.41 97.26 4.71	2 4.67 1.53 .12 2.74 1.94	73 4.53
School #9	24 29.95 1.18 1.49 75.00 1.59	8 2.05 17.31 .50 25.00 7.77	32 1.99
School #10	161 159.12 .02 10.00 94.71 10.68	9 10.88 .32 .56 5.29 8.74	170 10.56

Table 12--continued

Frequency Expected Cell Chi-Square Percent Row Percent Column Percent	High SES	Low SES	Total
School #11	152 154.44 .04 9.44 92.12 10.09	13 10.56 .56 .81 7.88 12.62	165 10.25
School #12	186 180.65 .16 11.55 96.37 12.34	7 12.35 2.31 .43 3.63 6.80	193 11.99
School #13	106 102.96 .09 6.58 96.36 7.03	4 7.04 1.31 .25 3.64 3.88	110 6.83
School #14	109 104.83 .16 6.77 97.32 7.23	3 7.16 2.42 .19 2.68 2.91	112 6.96
School #15	242 230.26 .60 15.03 98.37 16.06	4 15.74 8.75 .25 1.63 3.88	246 15.28

Table 12--continued

Frequency Expected Cell Chi-Square Percent Row Percent Column Percent	High SES	Low SES	Total
School #16	83 88.92 .39 5.16 87.37 5.51	12 6.08 5.77 .75 12.63 11.65	95 5.90
Total	1507 93.60	103 6.40	1610 100.00

Frequency Missing = 1

cell chi-square values in Table 12. An examination of these cell chi-square values revealed that schools 1, 3, 7, 9, 12, 14, 15, and 16 were contributing to the overall relationship. Schools 1, 3, 7, 9, and 16 were significantly more likely to have students in low-socioeconomic status than would be expected. Schools 12, 14, and 15 were significantly less likely to have low-socioeconomic students than would be expected.

An analysis of the significant relationship (chi-square = 9.88, with 1 d.f., $p < .00$) between socioeconomic status and gender is presented in Table 13. The overall chi-square value of 9.88 divided by 4 (i.e., the number of cells) established 2.47 as the significant cell chi-square value in Table 13. This value was present for this analysis between low-socioeconomic status and gender in that females were significantly less likely to be in low-socioeconomic status than would be expected and males were significantly more likely to be in low-socioeconomic status than would be expected.

Table 13

Chi-Square Test Comparing Socioeconomic Status (SES) by Gender

Frequency Expected Cell Chi-Square Percent Row Percent Column Percent	High SES	Low SES	Total
Female	797 781.58 .30 49.50 95.45 52.89	38 53.42 4.45 2.36 4.55 36.89	835 51.86
Male	710 725.42 .33 44.10 91.61 47.11	65 49.58 4.80 4.04 8.39 63.11	775 48.14
Total	1507 93.60	103 6.40	1610 100.00

Summary of Findings

The purpose of this study was to determine if race, gender, socioeconomic status, or school assignment taken independently as well as in combination were significant factors in predicting which students were assigned to the college preparatory mathematics track and which students were denied access to the college preparatory track. School assignment, socioeconomic status, and the combination of gender and socioeconomic status were found to be significantly related to students' placement into gatekeeper mathematics courses. Additionally, there was a strong association between race and placement into gatekeeper mathematics courses. However, the small numbers of students in the sample for certain races hindered an analysis for statistical significance.

CHAPTER 5

DISCUSSION

This study measured the assignment of gatekeeper mathematics courses against a meritocratic definition of fairness to determine if this process denied access to students from particular segments of society. Included in this final chapter are the study's principal findings, the relevance of the study's principal findings to meritocratic theory and to egalitarian theory, and the study's conclusions.

Principal Findings

In this study, school assignment, socioeconomic status, and the combination of gender and socioeconomic status were found to be significantly related to students' placement into gatekeeper mathematics. Therefore, the investigation into the following five research questions resulted in negative responses to questions 3, 4, and 5:

1. Were eighth-grade students who scored in the upper quartile in mathematics on a standardized achievement test scheduled into ninth-grade gatekeeper mathematics courses without regard to race?

2. Were eighth-grade students who scored in the upper quartile in mathematics on a standardized achievement test scheduled into ninth-grade gatekeeper mathematics courses without regard to gender?

3. Were eighth-grade students who scored in the upper quartile in mathematics on a standardized achievement test scheduled into ninth-grade gatekeeper mathematics courses without regard to socioeconomic status?

4. Were eighth-grade students who scored in the upper quartile in mathematics on a standardized achievement test scheduled into ninth-grade gatekeeper mathematics courses without regard to school assignment?

5. Were eighth-grade students who scored in the upper quartile in mathematics on a standardized achievement test scheduled into ninth-grade gatekeeper mathematics courses without regard to any combination of race, gender, socioeconomic status, or school assignment?

The following null hypotheses were rejected:

Ho_3: Socioeconomic status was not statistically significant in determining who had been denied admission to gatekeeper mathematics courses when academic ability was controlled.

Ho_4: School assignment was not statistically significant in determining who had been denied admission to gatekeeper mathematics courses when academic ability was controlled.

Ho_5: Any combination of race, gender, socioeconomic status, and/or school assignment was not statistically significant in determining who had been denied admission to gatekeeper mathematics courses when academic ability was controlled.

The findings of this study evinced that eighth-grade students who scored in the upper quartile in mathematics were not uniformly scheduled into the college preparatory mathematics track irrespective of their socioeconomic status, gender, or school assignment. Therefore, the admission of students to gatekeeper mathematics as measured in this study did not adhere to the meritocratic definition of fairness because admission into gatekeeper mathematics was denied for students from particular segments of society.

The negative response to research question 3 and the rejection of null hypothesis 3 resulted from the significant relationship between socioeconomic status and admission into gatekeeper mathematics. Low-socioeconomic students were three times more likely to be denied admission to gatekeeper mathematics courses than high-socioeconomic students (odds ratio = 3.21, significant at the .01 level).

The negative response to research question 4 and the rejection of the corresponding null hypothesis resulted from the statistically significant relationship found between school assignment and admission to gatekeeper mathematics courses. Schools with identifier numbers 2, 5, 7, 8, 10, 11, 13, and 15 were significantly more likely to place students into gatekeeper mathematics courses than reference school 16.

The logistic regression analyses of the main effects of gender and socioeconomic status was the only combination that contributed to a negative response to research question

5 and the rejection of the corresponding null hypothesis. High-socioeconomic males were found to be 77 percent less likely to be placed into gatekeeper mathematics than low-socioeconomic females (odds ratio = .23, significant at the .003 level), once the effects of gender and socioeconomic status were taken into account.

Additionally, the analysis of variance conducted between the controlled variable of academic ability and the predictor variables resulted in three significant relationships. Academic ability as measured by one of three CTBS mathematics subtests was found to be significantly related to school assignment for all three subtests, the total mathematics score was related to race, and the mathematics computation score was related to the combination of race and socioeconomic status.

In the present study, only students who scored in the upper quartile on the Comprehensive Test of Basic Skills were used in the analysis. The purpose of focusing on this select population was an attempt to control for the effects of differential mathematics achievement levels. Nevertheless, because mathematics variance persisted in this upper quartile, and the analysis of variance results showed a relationship between prior mathematics achievement and demographic variables in the logistic model, the attempt to control for a level of mathematics achievement by selection alone was imperfect. For this reason, a second logistic regression analysis was conducted using the total mathematics achievement score as a covariate in the regression model. Results from this analysis changed only slightly from the results of the initial model.

Relevance of Principal Findings to Meritocratic Theory

Central to a meritocracy is the premise that opportunities should be unrelated to race, gender, socioeconomic status, or school assignment. Curriculum placement should be based solely on individual merit, otherwise a meritocracy is not in operation. The presence of a significant relationship between the predictor variables of socioeconomic status, school assignment, and the combination of gender and socioeconomic status and the criterion variable of gatekeeper mathematics course placement was unexpected for educators who advocate that the current scheduling procedure adheres to meritocratic principles in the assignment of curriculum opportunities. A meritocrat would have anticipated a high placement rate for the students in this study because the sample included only students with proven mathematical ability. A meritocracy demands that students with proven academic abilities be given access to the curriculum choices that afford the greatest opportunities, the college preparatory track (Bell, 1973; Brubacher, 1982; Giarelli & Webb, 1980). According to meritocratic principles, students in this sample should have been consistently placed into college preparatory mathematics, that is, Algebra I or Geometry. Since this did not occur, the meritocratic educator is left questioning the current scheduling procedure or searching for a rationale for the findings.

A meritocrat's rationale could take the form of one of two arguments in an effort to place into credible context the significant and negative relationship between socioeconomic status and gatekeeper mathematics placement. First, a probable argument might be that the low-socioeconomic status students were denied gatekeeper mathematics placement because these students had less measured academic ability. However, even though there were varying degrees of academic ability that contributed to this relationship, the variability was confined to the category of high academic ability (the upper quartile).

A second plausible explanation might be that children with lower socioeconomic status have lower aspirations and less motivation to enter the college preparatory track. A point of contention could be argued that an equal opportunity meritocratic scheduling process was in place, but the placement was not sought or was subsequently refused. The logic would follow that course selections were stratified because of the depressed motivation of low-socioeconomic students and not as a result of the behavior of gatekeepers. There has been considerable research to validate the argument that socioeconomic status affects ambition (Garza & McNeal, 1988; Litten, 1982; Slavin, 1988; Slavin, 1987). Lower socioeconomic students tend to have less support and encouragement from outside the school setting to help them toward higher aspirations. For students from low-income families, the school counselor is particularly important in the academic counseling process because parents are less able to assist the students. Students from low-income families, African American students, and students who have parents with less education are more likely to rely on the school counselor for academic advice (Lee & Ekstrom, 1987; Oakes, 1990a; Litten, 1982, p. 91). Research by Garza & McNeal (1988) stated that even the support offered to students by school personnel paralleled the socioeconomic class level of the student.

> Students from an upper socioeconomic background tend to have more exploratory interviews with their counselors. They tend to be more expressive of their needs, are more egocentric, and are able to establish long-range goals, due to their upbringing. Middle class background students tend to seek counselor advice or help more frequently and for a longer period of time. . . . A disproportionately larger number of minority students are found in the lower socioeconomic class. Most students coming from a lower socioeconomic background tend to be concerned with survival and expect immediate advice and suggestions from the counselor. (p. 8)

In Beymer's (1989) profile of the student with high aspirations and motivation, socioeconomic status was a prominant factor. In his three-year study involving middle school students in Indiana, he found that students who felt they had the widest range of career possibilities shared the following characteristics:

- a positive sense of personal worth and self-esteem,
- able to process career and personal information in a complex manner,

- female, and
- from a middle-class family that includes both parents. (1989, p. 6)

A meritocracy demands access based on merit, and the position that access based on academic ability may have been offered but low student aspirations intervened could arguably succeed as a line of reasoning. It is a weakness of this study that this line of reasoning cannot be clearly substantiated or refuted. However, it is not the usual practice to give eighth-grade students decision-making power in their curriculum placement. It is true that students or parents can request a lower or higher level course, but it is the counselor, and to a lesser degree the teacher, who determines curriculum paths. The exceptions to this practice are few, but unfortunately, the exact numbers are not verifiable.

Meritocratic educators would applaud the absence of a relationship between gatekeeper mathematics and race. Stratifying opportunities by race is generally considered the most prevalent and insidious of inequitable practices. The fact that there were no statistically significant relationships involving any of the five races of this study and gatekeeper mathematics could be touted as evidence that a meritocracy was in operation for the scheduling procedure and affirmation that curriculum decisions were made in accordance with meritocratic principles and were free from invidious distinctions.

The meritocratic educator would laud the scheduling process for these students as free of injurious racial bias and would note that the one significant relationship involving gender bias was between the combination of males and socioeconomic status. High-socioeconomic males, thought to enjoy greater social privilege, were less likely than low-socioeconomic females to be placed into gatekeeper mathematics once the effects for gender and socioeconomic status were accounted for in the analysis. This is an unexpected finding, for the prevalent assumption would be that if a significant and negative relationship was found, it would be for low-socioeconomic African American females and males. Although the direction of the relationship for high-socioeconomic males runs counter to meritocratic thought, it represents a shift in the social order, a recodification that no longer spells automatic equity for high-socioeconomic males. The meritocratic educator would not be happy with this negative relationship but would be pleased that the relationship was not against those members of society generally thought to be the most disadvantaged.

The significant relationship between school assignment and gatekeeper mathematics requires a closer examination. The negative response to research question 4 would not greatly disturb the meritocratic educator because the statistical measurement was found to be in the positive direction, i.e., determining which schools were more likely to place students into gatekeeper mathematics as compared to the reference school. An examination between school assignments and gatekeeper mathematics placement added credibility to the meritocratic scheduling process. Schools 7 and 9, the schools in the study with the highest minority populations (99 percent each), were more likely to place students into gatekeeper mathematics than the reference school (odds ratio 5.08 and 2.39 respectively). This was another affirmation for the meritocratic educator that the scheduling process was functioning equitably.

Relevance of Principal Findings to Egalitarian Theory

Egalitarians would expect that race, gender, socioeconomic status, and school assignment would be significant predictors of who would be denied admission into gatekeeper mathematics. The expectations held by egalitarians were partially supported in this study in that a significant relationship was found to exist between the placement of students into gatekeeper mathematics courses and a student's gender, socioeconomic status, and school assignment.

The findings of this study substantiated the concern of egalitarians that learning opportunities are stratified by socioeconomic status. The negative response to question 3 and the rejection of the corresponding null hypothesis would be expected. Egalitarians have argued that low-socioeconomic students are less likely to be placed into college preparatory courses (George, 1988; Lee & Ekstrom,

1987). The high-socioeconomic students of this study were
three times more likely to be placed into gatekeeper
mathematics courses than low-socioeconomic students.

The egalitarians consider the socioeconomic status of a
school as a stratifier of opportunities. Oakes (1990a)
observed that students attending high-socioeconomic schools
have far greater opportunities to take critical gatekeeper
mathematics courses that will prepare them for advanced
mathematics courses than students in low-socioeconomic and
high minority schools.

> Fewer schools serving low-income and minority students
> offer the opportunity to begin the college-preparatory
> mathematics sequence. . . . Among schools that offer
> these courses, the proportion of students who take them
> . . . is far greater at high-income and predominantly
> white schools. These findings are quite disturbing
> . . . . They strongly signal unequal access to valuable
> science and mathematics knowledge. (p. 42)

This study's findings both support and refute the
egalitarians's position as outlined by Oakes. The
socioeconomic status of students was indeed tied to
gatekeeper mathematics course placement, but the
socioeconomic status of a school and the high minority
composition of a school did not support the egalitarian
position that the presence of these two conditions adversely
stratified opportunities in the college preparatory
mathematics track.

The argument that schools with a predominance of low-
socioeconomic students are less likely to offer gatekeeper
mathematics was examined in the five schools that were
significantly more likely to have students in low-

socioeconomic status. Three schools (1, 3, 16) supported the argument, while schools 7 and 9 dramatically contradicted this position. Schools 7 and 9 are the predominant minority schools for the school system of this study, both having an African American population of 99 percent (Table 14) and both having a high rate of placement into gatekeeper mathematics. School 7 had the highest likelihood for scheduling students into gatekeeper mathematics, at five times more likely than the least likely reference school 16. School 9 was two and one-half times more likely to schedule students into gatekeeper mathematics courses. Therefore, the socioeconomic status of the schools in this study and admission to gatekeeper mathematics were not consistently related in the direction of egalitarian argument, with two of the five lowest socioeconomic schools anchoring both ends of the range; school 16 was the least likely to admit and school 7 the most likely to admit.

Also, a contradiction existed in the egalitarians' argument that high minority schools were less likely to offer college preparatory courses. All five of the schools with the least likely rate of gatekeeper course placement (school 1, 3, 6, 12, 16) are predominately white schools; school 16 (which is the least likely to place students into gatekeeper mathematics courses) is 66.9 percent white, school 1 is 54.5 percent white, school 3 is 87.9 percent white, school 6 is 60.7 percent white, and school 12 is 74.2 percent white (Table 14).

Table 14

Percent of 1993-1994 Ethnic Enrollment by School

School Indentifier Number	African Americans	Asians	Hispanics	Native Americans	Whites
1	37.9	4.8	2.7	.1	54.5
2	86.8	.1	.2	.1	12.5
3	10.5	.8	.8	-	87.9
4	74.2	.7	.3	-	24.8
5	21.5	2.6	2.5	.3	73.2
6	29.2	4.7	5.3	.1	60.7
7	99.0	-	-	-	1.0
8	16.0	.9	1.3	-	81.9
9	99.6	.1	-	-	.4
10	13.7	5.1	2.7	-	78.5
11	30.9	4.0	1.9	.2	63.0
12	15.3	7.7	2.6	.2	74.2
13	25.2	7.4	5.0	.1	62.3
14	29.5	2.5	2.3	.2	65.6
15	14.6	2.2	1.8	.3	81.1
16	32.2	.4	.5	.1	66.9

Source: Student Information Management Systems for this School System, 1994

Additionally, egalitarians have argued that opportunities are skewed based on a student's gender, with males having the greater opportunities for accessing college preparatory courses (Bowles & Gintis, 1976). The rejection of null hypothesis 5 supported this position in that males were found to be two times more likely to be scheduled into gatekeeper mathematics courses than females. However, the interaction of gender in combination with socioeconomic status did not follow the predictable course. High-socioeconomic males were scheduled into gatekeeper mathematics courses at only 23 percent the rate of low-socioeconomic females. This was an unexpected finding because males were more likely to be scheduled into gatekeeper mathematics courses and high-socioeconomic students were more likely to be scheduled into gatekeeper mathematics courses.

According to the principles of a meritocracy, school personnel act fairly toward students when they offer curriculum opportunities based on academic skills and achievements (Brubacher, 1982). Counselors place students in curriculum courses based on academic abilities determined by standardized test scores that are considered to be valid and reliable measures. Access to the college preparatory mathematics track is given to students with the highest academic ability as demonstrated on valid and reliable measures. For the school counselor, who has the primary responsibility for placing students in mathematics courses, factors such as race, gender, socioeconomic status, and school assignment should be extraneous to the determination of course placement.

Egalitarians take issue with the placement of students in mathematics courses based on standardized tests. The distribution of academic resources based on standardized test results is an unfair practice, they believe, because standardized tests are biased in favor of students with social privilege (Archbald & Newman, 1988; Wilkerson, 1982). Achievement often seems to operate as a stratifier of opportunity dependent on race, gender, behavior, or social class, raising the question of discriminatory and unequal rather than educational opportunity (Archbald & Newman, 1988; Page, 1991, Wilkerson, 1982). This study's findings supported the concern of egalitarians that standardized test results are related to social privilege. School assignments, race, and the combination of race and socioeconomic status were all significantly related to academic ability as determined by CTBS mathematics subtests scores.

Egalitarians have expressed concern that opportunities for mathematics are disproportionately skewed based on a student's race. National statistics on academic achievement, high school completion, acquisition of college degrees, and occupational status and income reveal inequities in the accomplishments and representation of racial and ethnic minorities in mathematics and science attainments (Oakes, 1990a, 1990b). This study did not find any statistically significant relationships between race and placement into gatekeeper mathematics courses. However, two strong associations were found and deserve discussion. The Asian race was found to be seven times more likely to be placed into gatekeeper mathematics courses than the white race, and the African American race was less likely to be placed into gatekeeper mathematics courses, at 85 percent the rate of white students.

Conclusions and Recommendations

The American public school system promises an open society in which students have a free and equal opportunity to achieve success. The gatekeeper scheduling process is central to the debate about equal access to effective educational resources for all students. On one side of this debate are meritocratic educators who maintain that students who are denied entrance into gatekeeper mathematics courses based on an objective measure of academic ability have been treated fairly. The placement decision was made on the basis of an objective measure and not on information extraneous to academic ability, such as the fact that the student is a member of a particular segment of society. On the other side of the debate are egalitarians who claim that variables related to social privilege, such as race, gender, socioeconomic status, and school assignment, are factors in determining who is allowed access to the gatekeeper mathematics courses. Also at issue for egalitarians is the question of equity in determining curriculum opportunities based on individual academic achievement when measured by even the least biased testing procedures. Egalitarians maintain that testing favors students of social privilege and that testing procedures do not give information about how particular children will perform in particular classrooms, about their willingness to engage, or about their compensating for untested abilities (Page, 1991).

The research on equity in curriculum placement fails to settle this debate. This study was committed to examining the gatekeeper mathematics process in such a way as to add to an understanding of the meritocracy of curriculum placement procedures. This study satisfied this commitment by examining which students were given access to gatekeeper mathematics. Analysis of this study's results demonstrated that educational opportunities for the students of this sample were related to economic standing, the combination of gender and socioeconomic status, and school assignment.

A strong association was present between socioeconomic status and placement into gatekeeper mathematics. High-socioeconomic students were three times more likely than low-socioeconomic students to be placed into gatekeeper mathematics. It should be reiterated at this point that low-socioeconomic students comprised only a small percentage of the sample (six percent, or 103, out of 1611 students). A large number of these low-socioeconomic students (36) were denied admission into gatekeeper mathematics.

The argument that low-socioeconomic students took themselves out of the college preparatory track is possible but not probable. The contention that low-socioeconomic students experience a lack of motivation is supported in the literature, but the scheduling procedures in place for the students in this study curtailed their choices of curriculum paths and, therefore, eliminated motivation as a factor.

High-socioeconomic males were less likely than low-socioeconomic females to be placed into gatekeeper mathematics once the effects for gender and socioeconomic status were taken into account. This was an unexpected finding because high-socioeconomic males are generally considered to enjoy greater social privilege.

The relationship between school assignment and gatekeeper mathematics was perhaps the most revealing. It was apparent from the findings of this study that opportunities for students to take the college preparatory mathematics curriculum were contingent on a student's school assignment. It was not the high minority schools, but the predominantly white schools, in which curriculum opportunities were adversely stratified.

This study did not produce the expected results for either the meritocratic position or the egalitarian position. Predictions by egalitarians were unfounded in that opportunities were not adversely stratified for minorities, females, students from high minority schools, or students from low-socioeconomic schools. The categories least likely to be of concern to egalitarians, i.e., the predominately white school and high-socioeconomic males, were the variables that significantly and negatively stratified educational opportunities. Opportunities were not determined by a student's individual achievement, as a meritocracy demands, but were dependent on a student's school assignment and socioeconomic status.

"Research has helped school people realize not only that equity is a moral obligation of schools, but that student learning and achievement are highly related to equitable practices" (Shakeshaft, 1990, p. 213). Educators need to understand equity issues and be prepared to identify and eliminate institutional practices that deter equity.

Student success is largely dependent on the initiative of the individual student, but there are curriculum enrollment patterns that can have a profound effect on the opportunity for student success. Mathematics underachievement continues to be the largest separating factor in student success. Mathematics is the gateway subject that largely determines future academic study. For example, scores on the Scholastic Assessment Test (SAT) are directly correlated to course work in mathematics, and such course work, in turn, is related to successfully completing Algebra I by the end of grade nine (Montgomery County Public Schools, 1994; Dade County Public Schools, 1994).

In order to address institutional practices that deter access to gatekeeper mathematics, a systemwide plan is needed to examine the policies that govern curriculum tracking. This plan should include broad system-wide strategies as well as specific tasks for school personnel and district level administrators. Strategies might include the following recommendations:

1. Provide staff development to help educators understand the philosophical and societal issues involved in educational equity. Teach educators, parents, and communities to identify school practices that adversely stratify educational opportunities. Organize strategies and tasks to support success for each student. Clearly define how to address the disparity in educational access.

2. Encourage and support students to change their perceptions of the relationship between educational achievement and the opportunities and rewards available in society.

3. Provide students with timely information and guidance to take challenging courses that will prepare them for postsecondary education, employment, or both.

4. Provide a comprehensive system-wide database on student progress that will facilitate effective school and system-wide monitoring of important indicators of student progress and success.

5. Provide opportunities in PreK-8 pre-algebra mathematics and require the completion of Algebra I and Geometry for graduation.

6.   Strengthen the content and instruction of mathematics course work to enhance student learning through challenging standards (Dade County Public Schools, 1994; Montgomery County Public Schools, 1994).

We are faced with a need to prepare all students for a society that will be unlike any that has come before us. The time has passed when Americans can be satisfied that only a select few are challenged to pursue the study of mathematics. We can no longer assign each student to a predictable category of achievement and employment. We must prepare all students to apply mathematical knowledge. So we need to ensure that all of our students have access to the information and experiences that will allow them to understand and influence the society of the future.

LOGISTIC REGRESSION ANALYSIS
OF ALL MAIN AND INTERACTIVE
PREDICTOR VARIABLES

Table 1-A

Logistic Regression Analysis of Maximum Likelihood Estimates
of Predictor Variables on Gatekeeper Mathematics Placement

Effect	Wald Chi-Square	Standard Error	Pr > Chi Square	Odds Ratio
A	2.74	1.19	.10	7.19
AA	.11	.51	.74	.85
H	1.00	1.37	.32	3.93
M	3.58	.49	.06	2.54
A*M	3.65	1.24	.06	.09
AA*M	2.61	.32	.11	.59
H*M	1.19	.84	.28	.40
HSES	6.29	.46	.01*	3.21
HSES*A	1.68	1.07	.20	3.98
HSES*AA	.09	.50	.76	.86
HSES*H	1.18	1.27	.28	.25
HSES*M	8.83	.49	.00*	.23
S1	.38	.36	.54	1.25

Table 1-A--continued

Effect	Wald Chi-Square	Standard Error	Pr > Chi Square	Odds Ratio
S2	4.27	.47	.04*	2.64
S3	.02	.62	.88	1.10
S4	2.57	.81	.11	3.69
S5	10.50	.28	.00*	2.46
S6	.11	.31	.74	1.11
S7	6.72	.63	.01*	5.09
S8	8.94	.37	.00*	3.02
S9	3.35	.48	.07	2.39
S10	11.87	.29	.00*	2.69
S11	15.11	.29	.00*	3.12
S12	.94	.27	.33	1.30
S13	6.18	.31	.01*	2.17
S14	3.31	.30	.07	1.74
S15	10.84	.26	.00*	2.38

Note: A = Asians; AA = African Americans; H = Hispanics; M = Males; HSES = High-socioeconomic Status; S = School; * = Statistically Significant

Table 2-A

Logistic Regression Analysis of Maximum Likelihood Estimates of Predictor Variables (Including Total Mathematics as a Covariate) on Gatekeeper Mathematics Placement

Predictor	Standard Error	Wald Chi-Square	Pr> Chi-Square	Odds Ratio
A	1.20	1.43	.23	4.21
AA	.54	.41	.52	.71
H	1.41	.94	.33	3.95
M	.52	1.60	.20	1.94
A*M	1.28	3.25	.07	.10
AA*M	.34	2.08	.14	.62
H*M	.89	1.13	.28	.39
HSES	.51	2.07	.15	2.07
HSES*A	1.13	2.78	.09	6.54
HSES*AA	.53	.17	.67	1.24
HSES*H	1.29	.82	.36	.31
HSES*M	.52	4.94	.02*	.31
S1	.38	.87	.34	1.43
S2	.48	3.83	.05*	2.56
S3	.65	.01	.94	1.05

Table 2-A--continued

Predictor	Standard Error	Wald Chi-Square	Pr> Chi-Square	Odds Ratio
S4	.83	1.57	.21	2.84
S5	.29	5.81	.01*	2.02
S6	.32	.14	.70	1.13
S7	.64	7.11	.00*	5.57
S8	.41	9.25	.00*	3.42
S9	.50	2.59	.10	2.23
S10	.31	9.42	.00*	2.58
S11	.31	11.23	.00*	2.78
S12	.28	.14	.71	1.11
S13	.33	6.51	.01*	2.30
S14	.32	3.30	.06	1.78
S15	.28	6.64	.01*	2.04

Note: A = Asians; AA = African Americans; H = Hispanics; M = Males; HSES = High-socioeconomic Status; S = School; * = Statistically Significant. An odds ratio ≥ 1.0 has a greater likelihood for admission to gatekeeper mathematics courses than the reference group. An odds ratio <1.0 means that there is less likelihood for admission.

FREQUENCY AND PERCENT TABLES OF
GATEKEEPER MATHEMATICS ADMISSIONS OF
ALL MAIN AND INTERACTIVE PREDICTOR VARIABLES

Table 1-B

Frequency and Percent of Gatekeeper Mathematics and
Race

Frequency Percent Row Percent Column Percent	Admitted to Gatekeeper Mathematics	Denied Gatekeeper Mathematics	Total
Asian	79 4.90 89.77 6.71	9 .56 10.23 2.08	88 5.46
African American	156 9.68 64.46 13.24	86 5.34 35.54 19.86	242 15.02
Hispanic	20 1.24 62.50 1.70	12 .75 37.50 2.77	32 1.99
Native American	3 .19 75.00 .25	1 .06 25.00 .23	4 .25
White	920 57.11 73.90 78.10	325 20.17 26.10 75.06	1245 77.28
Total	1178 73.12	433 26.88	1611

Table 2-B

<u>Frequency and Percent of Gatekeeper Mathematics and</u>
<u>Gender</u>

Frequency Percent Row Percent Column Percent	Admitted to Gatekeeper Mathematics	Denied Gatekeeper Mathematics	Totals
Female	656 40.72 78.56 55.69	179 11.11 21.44 41.34	835 51.83
Male	522 32.40 67.27 44.31	254 15.77 32.73 58.66	776 48.17
Total	1178 73.12	433 26.88	1611 100.00

Table 3-B

Frequency and Percent of Admissions to Gatekeeper
Mathematics and Gender by Race

Race	Gender		
Frequency Percent Row Percent Column Percent	Female	Male	Total
Asian	42 3.57 53.16 6.40	37 3.14 46.84 7.09	79 6.71
African American	92 7.81 58.97 14.02	64 5.43 41.03 12.26	156 13.24
Hispanic	10 .85 50.00 1.52	10 .85 50.00 1.92	20 1.70
Native American	2 .17 66.67 .30	1 .08 33.33 .19	3 .25
White	510 43.29 55.43 77.74	410 34.80 44.57 78.54	920 78.10
Total	656 55.69	522 44.31	1178 100.00

Table 4-B

Frequency and Percent of Denial of Gatekeeper
Mathematics and Gender by Race

Race	Gender		
Frequency Percent Row Percent Column Percent	Female	Male	Total
Asian	1 .23 11.11 .56	8 1.85 88.89 3.15	9 2.08
African American	34 7.85 39.53 18.99	52 12.01 60.47 20.47	86 19.86
Hispanic	3 .69 25.00 1.68	9 2.08 75.00 3.54	12 2.77
Native American	0 .00 .00 .00	1 .23 100.00 .39	1 .23
White	141 32.56 43.38 78.77	184 42.49 56.62 72.44	325 75.06
Total	179 41.34	254 58.66	433 100.00

Table 5-B

<u>Frequency and Percent of Gatekeeper Mathematics and
Socioeconomic Status (SES)</u>

Frequency Percent Row Percent Column Percent	Admitted to Gatekeeper Mathematics	Denied Gatekeeper Mathematics	Total
High SES	1111 69.00 94.31 73.72	396 24.60 91.67 26.28	1507
Low SES	67 4.16 5.69 65.5	36 2.24 8.33 34.95	103
Total	1178 93.60	432 6.40	1610 100.00

Frequency Missing = 1

Table 6-B

<u>Frequency and Percent of Admissions into Gatekeeper</u>
<u>Mathematics and Socioeconomic Status (SES) by Race</u>

Race	SES		
Frequency Percent Row Percent Column Percent	High SES	Low SES	Total
Asian	72 6.11 91.14 6.48	7 .59 8.86 10.45	79 6.71
African American	133 11.29 85.26 11.97	23 1.95 14.74 34.33	156 13.24
Hispanic	16 1.36 80.00 1.44	4 .34 20.00 5.97	20 1.70
Native American	3 .25 100.00 .27	0 .00 .00 .00	3 .25
White	887 75.30 96.41 79.84	33 2.80 3.59 49.25	920 78.10
Total	1111 94.31	67 5.69	1178 100.00

Table 7-B

Frequency and Percent of Denial of Gatekeeper
Mathematics and Socioeconomic Status (SES) by Race

Race		SES	
Frequency Percent Row Percent Column Percent	High SES	Low SES	Total
Asian	7 1.62 77.78 1.77	2 .46 22.22 5.56	9 2.08
African American	68 15.74 80.00 17.17	17 3.94 20.00 47.22	85 19.68
Hispanic	11 2.55 91.67 2.78	1 .23 8.33 2.78	12 2.78
Native American	1 .23 100.00 .25	0 .00 .00 .00	1 .23
White	309 71.53 95.08 78.03	16 3.70 4.92 44.44	325 75.23
Total	396 91.67	36 8.33	432 100.00

Frequency Missing = 1

Table 8-B

<u>Frequency and Percent of Admission into Gatekeeper</u>
<u>Mathematics and Socioeconomic Status (SES) by Gender</u>

Race	Gender		
Frequency Percent Row Percent Column Percent	Female	Male	Total
High SES	634 53.82 57.07 96.65	477 40.49 42.93 91.38	1111 94.31
Low SES	22 1.87 32.84 3.35	45 3.82 67.16 8.62	67 5.69
Total	656 55.69	522 44.31	1178 100.00

Table 9-B

<u>Frequency and Percent of Denial of Gatekeeper</u>
<u>Mathematics and Socioeconomic Status (SES) by Gender</u>

Race	Gender		
Frequency Percent Row Percent Column Percent	Female	Male	Total
High SES	163 37.73 41.16 91.06	233 53.94 58.84 92.09	396 91.67
Low SES	16 3.70 44.44 8.94	20 4.63 55.56 7.91	36 8.33
Total	179 41.44	253 58.56	432 100.00

Frequency Missing = 1

Table 10-B

<u>Frequency and Percent of Gatekeeper Mathematics and</u>
<u>School Assignment</u>

Frequency Percent Row Percent Column Percent	Admitted to Gatekeeper Mathematics	Denied Gatekeeper Mathematics	Total
School #1	35 2.17 64.81 2.97	19 1.18 35.19 4.39	54 3.35
School #2	23 1.43 71.88 1.95	9 .56 28.12 2.08	32 1.99
School #3	8 .50 61.54 .68	5 .31 38.46 1.15	13 .81
School #4	11 .68 84.62 .01	2 .12 15.38 .46	13 .81
School #5	146 9.06 77.25 12.39	43 2.67 22.75 9.93	189 11.73

Table 10-B--continued

Frequency Percent Row Percent Column Percent	Admitted to Gatekeeper Mathematics	Denied Gatekeeper Mathematics	Total
School #6	58 3.60 61.70 4.92	36 2.24 38.30 8.31	94 5.83
School #7	16 .99 80.00 1.36	4 .25 20.00 .92	20 1.24
School #8	59 3.66 80.82 5.01	14 .87 19.18 3.23	73 4.53
School #9	22 1.37 68.75 1.87	10 .62 31.25 2.31	32 1.99
School #10	134 8.32 78.82 11.38	36 2.24 21.28 8.31	170 10.55
School #11	132 8.19 80.00 11.21	33 2.05 20.00 7.62	165 10.24

Table 10-B--continued

Frequency Percent Row Percent Column Percent	Admitted to Gatekeeper Mathematics	Denied Gatekeeper Mathematics	Total
School #12	129 8.01 66.84 10.95	64 3.97 33.16 14.70	193 11.98
School #13	82 5.09 74.55 6.96	28 1.74 25.45 6.47	110 6.83
School #14	79 4.90 70.54 6.71	33 2.05 29.46 7.62	112 6.95
School #15	189 11.73 76.83 16.04	57 3.54 23.17 13.16	246 15.27
School #16	55 3.41 57.89 4.67	40 2.48 42.11 9.24	95 5.90
Total	1178 73.12	433 26.88	1611

Table 11-B

Frequency and Percent of Race (African Americans) by
School Assignment and Admissions to Gatekeeper
Mathematics

Frequency Percent Row Percent Column Percent	Admitted to Gatekeeper Mathematics	Denied Gatekeeper Mathematics	Total
School #1	2 .83 40.00 1.28	3 1.24 60.00 3.53	5 2.08
School #2	15 6.22 68.18 9.62	7 2.90 31.82 8.24	22 9.13
School #3	0 .00 .00 .00	0 .00 .00 .00	0 .00
School #4	6 2.49 100.00 3.85	0 .00 .00 .00	6 2.50
School #5	11 4.56 57.89 7.05	8 3.32 42.11 9.41	19 7.88

Table 11-B--continued

Frequency Percent Row Percent Column Percent	Admitted to Gatekeeper Mathematics	Denied Gatekeeper Mathematics	Total
School #6	3 1.45 37.50 1.92	5 2.05 62.50 5.88	8 3.32
School #7	16 6.64 84.21 10.26	3 1.25 15.79 3.53	19 7.88
School #8	5 2.05 50.00 3.21	5 2.05 50.00 5.88	10 4.15
School #9	21 8.71 67.74 13.46	10 4.15 32.26 11.76	31 12.86
School #10	8 3.32 57.14 5.13	6 2.49 42.86 7.06	14 5.81
School #11	23 9.54 69.70 14.74	10 4.15 30.30 11.76	33 13.69

Table 11-B--continued

Frequency Percent Row Percent Column Percent	Admitted to Gatekeeper Mathematics	Denied Gatekeeper Mathematics	Total
School #12	9 3.73 64.29 5.77	5 2.05 35.71 5.88	14 5.81
School #13	12 4.98 70.59 7.69	5 2.05 29.41 5.88	17 7.05
School #14	6 2.49 54.55 3.85	5 2.05 45.45 5.88	11 4.56
School #15	14 5.80 70.00 8.97	6 2.49 30.00 7.07	20 8.30
School #16	5 2.05 41.67 3.20	7 2.90 58.33 8.24	12 4.98
Total	156 100.00	85 100.00	241 100.00

Table 12-B

Frequency and Percent of Race (Asians) by School
Assignment and Admissions to Gatekeeper Mathematics

Frequency Percent Row Percent Column Percent	Admitted to Gatekeeper Mathematics	Denied Gatekeeper Mathematics	Total
School #1	4 4.54 100.00 5.06	0 .00 .00 .00	4 4.54
School #2	0 .00 .00 .00	0 .00 .00 .00	0 .00
School #3	1 1.14 100.00 1.27	0 .00 .00 .00	1 1.14
School #4	1 1.14 100.00 1.27	0 .00 .00 .00	1 1.14
School #5	9 10.23 90.00 11.39	1 1.14 10.00 11.11	10 11.36

Table 12-B--continued

Frequency Percent Row Percent Column Percent	Admitted to Gatekeeper Mathematics	Denied Gatekeeper Mathematics	Total
School #6	5 5.68 100.00 6.33	0 .00 .00 .00	5 5.68
School #7	0 .00 .00 .00	0 .00 .00 .00	0 .00
School #8	1 1.14 100.00 1.27	0 .00 .00 .00	1 1.14
School #9	0 .00 .00 .00	0 .00 .00 .00	0 .00
School #10	12 13.64 100.00 15.19	0 .00 .00 .00	12 13.64
School #11	4 4.54 100.00 5.06	0 .00 .00 .00	4 4.54

Table 12-B--continued

Frequency Percent Row Percent Column Percent	Admitted to Gatekeeper Mathematics	Denied Gatekeeper Mathematics	Total
School #12	19 21.59 73.08 24.05	7 7.95 26.92 77.78	26 29.55
School #13	9 10.23 90.00 11.39	1 1.14 10.00 11.11	10 11.36
School #14	8 9.09 100.00 10.13	0 .00 .00 .00	8 9.09
School #15	6 6.82 100.00 7.59	0 .00 .00 .00	6 6.82
School #16	0 .00 .00 .00	0 .00 .00 .00	0 .00
Total	79 100.00	9 100.00	88 100.00

Table 13-B

Frequency and Percent of Race (White) by School
Assignment and Admissions to Gatekeeper Mathematics

Frequency Percent Row Percent Column Percent	Admitted to Gatekeeper Mathematics	Denied Gatekeeper Mathematics	Total
School #1	28 2.25 63.64 3.04	16 1.28 36.36 4.92	44 3.53
School #2	8 .64 80.00 .87	2 .16 20.00 .62	10 .80
School #3	7 .56 58.33 .76	5 .40 41.67 1.54	12 .96
School #4	4 .32 66.67 .44	2 .16 33.33 .62	6 .48
School #5	122 9.80 78.71 13.26	33 2.65 21.29 10.15	155 12.45

Table 13-B--continued

Frequency Percent Row Percent Column Percent	Admitted to Gatekeeper Mathematics	Denied Gatekeeper Mathematics	Total
School #6	50 4.02 65.79 5.44	26 2.09 34.21 8.00	76 6.10
School #7	0 .00 .00 .00	1 .08 100.00 .31	1 .08
School #8	50 4.02 84.75 5.43	9 .72 15.25 2.77	59 4.74
School #9	1 .08 100.00 .11	0 .00 .00 .00	1 .08
School #10	114 9.16 79.72 12.39	29 2.33 20.28 8.92	143 11.49
School #11	102 8.19 81.60 11.09	23 1.85 18.40 7.08	125 10.04

Table 13-B--continued

Frequency Percent Row Percent Column Percent	Admitted to Gatekeeper Mathematics	Denied Gatekeeper Mathematics	Total
School #12	97 7.79 65.99 10.54	50 4.02 34.01 15.39	147 11.81
School #13	58 4.66 74.36 6.30	20 1.61 25.64 6.15	78 6.27
School #14	62 4.98 71.26 6.74	25 2.01 28.74 7.69	87 6.99
School #15	168 13.49 76.71 18.26	51 4.10 23.29 15.69	219 17.59
School #16	49 3.93 59.76 5.33	33 2.65 40.24 10.15	82 6.59
Total	920 100.00	325 100.00	1245 100.00

REFERENCES

Agresti, A. (1990). <u>Categorical data analysis</u>. New York, NY: John Wiley & Sons.

Alexander, K. L., Cook, M., & McDill, E. L. (1978). Curriculum tracking and educational stratification: Some further evidence. <u>American Sociological Review</u>, <u>43</u> 47-66.

Archbald, D. A., & Newman, F. M. (1988). <u>Beyond standardized testing: Assessing authentic academic achievement in the secondary school</u>. Reston, VA: National Association of Secondary School Principals.

Bastian, A., Fruchter, N., Gittell, M., Greer, C., & Haskins, K. (1986). <u>Choosing equality</u>. Philadelphia, PA: Temple University Press.

Bell, D. (1973). <u>The coming of post-industrial society: A venture into social forecasting</u>. New York, NY: Basic Books, Inc.

Beymer, L. (1989). <u>Improving equity career guidance in Indiana junior high and middle schools: Results and recommendations from a three year project</u>. Indiana Commission on Vocational and Technical Education. Terre Haute, IN: Indiana State University.

Bowles, S., & Gintis, H. (1976). <u>Schooling in capitalist America</u>. New York, NY: Basic Books.

Brase, C. H., & Brase, C. P. (1991). <u>Understandable statistics</u>. Lexington, MA: D. C. Heath and Company.

Brubacher, J. S. (1982). <u>On the philosophy of higher education</u>. San Francisco, CA: Jossey-Bass.

Commission on Precollege Guidance and Counseling (1986). <u>Keeping the options open: Recommendations</u>. New York, NY: College Entrance Examination Board.

Dade County Public Schools (1994, January). <u>Improving science and mathematics for all students: An urban systemic initiative</u>. Paper presented to the National Science Foundation, Arlington, VA.

Fenwick, J. J. (1987). Caught in the middle. Educational reform for young adolescents in California public schools (Report No. ISBN-0-8011-0488-2). Los Angeles, CA: Bureau of Publications, California Department of Education. (ERIC Document Reproduction Service No. ED 289 246)

Gamoran, A. (1986). Instruction and institutional effects of ability grouping. Sociology of Education, 59, 185-198.

Gamoran, A. (1987). The stratification of high school learning opportunities. Sociology of Education, 60, 135-155.

Gamoran, A. (1990). Instructional organizational practices that affect equity. In H. P. Baptiste, H. C. Waxman, J. W. deFelix, & J. E. Anderson (Eds.). Leadership, equity, and school effectiveness (pp. 155-172). Newbury Park, CA: Sage Publications.

Gardner, J. W. (1961). Excellence. Can we be equal and excellent too? New York, NY: Harper & Row Publishers.

Garza, J. F., & McNeal, A. E. (1988). Equity in counseling and advising students: Keeping options open (Report No. UD 026 838-849). Columbus, OH: National Middle School Association. (ERIC Document Reproduction Service No. ED 322 233)

George, P. S. (1988). Tracking and ability grouping: Which way for the middle school? Middle School Journal, 20(1), 21-28.

Giarelli, J. M., & Webb, R. B. (1980). Higher education, meritocracy and distributive justice. Educational Studies: A Journal in the Foundations of Education, 11, 221-238.

Good, T. L., & Brophy, J. E. (1987). Looking in classrooms (2nd ed.). New York, NY: Harper & Row.

Jencks, C., Smith, M., Acland, H., Bane, M., Cohen, D., Gintis, H., Heynes, B., & Michelson, S. (1972). Inequality: A reassessment of the effect of family and schooling in America. New York, NY: Basic Books.

Kozol, J. (1991). Savage inequalities: Children in America's schools. New York, NY: Crown Publishers, Inc.

Lee, V. E., & Ekstrom, R. B. (1987). Student access to guidance counseling in high school. American Educational Research Journal, 24, 287-310.

Litten, L. (1982). Different strokes in the applicant pool: Some refinements in a model of student college choice. The Journal of Higher Education, 53(4), 383-402.

McClelland, K. (1990). Cumulative disadvantage among the highly ambitious. Sociology of Education, 63 102-121.

Mendel, R., & Lincoln, C. (1991). Guiding children to success: What schools and communities can do. Chapel Hill, NC: MDC Incorporated. (ERIC Document Reproduction Service No. Ed 338 982)

Montgomery County Public Schools (1994, April). Success for every student plan. Paper presented to the National Science Foundation, Arlington, VA.

Oakes, J. (1990a). Multiplying inequalities: The effects of race, social class, and tracking on opportunities to learn mathematics and science. Santa Monica, CA: RAND Publications Department.

Oakes, J. (1990b). Keeping track. New Haven, CT: Yale University Press.

Page, R. (1991). Lower-track classrooms. New York, NY: Teachers College Press.

Pelavin, S., & Kane, M. (1990). Changing the odds: Factors increasing access to college. New York, NY: College Entrance Examination Board.

Preer, J. L. (1981). Minority access to higher education. Washington, DC: American Association for Higher Education.

Purpel, D. E., & Shapiro, H. S. (1985). Schools and meaning. Lanham, MD: University Press of America.

Rehberg, R. A., & Rosenthal, E. R. (1978). Class and merit in the American high school: An assessment of the revisionist and meritocratic arguments. New York: Longman.

Rich, J. M., & DeVitis, J. L. (1992). Competition in education. Springfield, IL: Thomas Books.

Rosenbaum, J. E. (1976). Making inequality: The hidden curriculum of high school tracking. New York, NY: Wiley.

Shakeshaft, C. (1990). Administrative preparation for equity. In H. P. Baptiste, H. C. Waxman, J. W. deFelix, & J. E. Anderson (Eds.), Leadership, equity, and school effectiveness (pp. 213-223). Newbury Park, CA: Sage Publications.

Slavin, R. E. (1987). Ability grouping and student achievement in elementary schools: A best-evidence synthesis. Review of Educational Research, 57, 293-336.

Slavin, R. E. (1988). Synthesis of research on grouping in elementary and secondary schools. Educational Leadership, 46, 67-77.

Strike, K. (1982). Educational policy and the just society. Urbana, IL: University of Illinois Press.

Turner, F. J. (1903). Contributions of the west to American democracy. Atlantic Monthly, 91(543), 83-87.

Webb, R. B., & Sherman, R. R. (1989). Schooling and society (2nd ed.). New York, NY: Macmillan Publishing Company.

Wilkerson, M. (1982). The mask of meritocracy and egalitarianism. Educational Record, 63(1), 4-11.

BIOGRAPHICAL SKETCH

Carolyn Stone was born in Mobile, Alabama, on January 11, 1950, the third of Elsie and Silas Bishop's six children. Mrs. Stone was raised in Mobile where she spent 17 years in the public school system, kindergarten through college. She received her B.S. degree in elementary education from the University of South Alabama in 1972. She received the Master of Arts in Counseling degree from the University of North Florida in 1981 and a Specialist in Education degree in guidance and counseling/school psychology from the University of Florida in 1985.

Mrs. Stone has been an educator in the Duval County School System in Jacksonville, Florida, for 22 years. She taught elementary school for nine years, served as an elementary counselor for four years, a high school counselor for five years, and a school psychologist intern for 1000 clock hours. Presently, Mrs. Stone is serving Northeast Florida as the Florida Department of Education's Guidance Counselor Consultant and since 1989 has been the Supervisor of Guidance Services for the elementary, middle, and high school counselors of the Duval County School System. In August, Mrs. Stone will begin work as an assistant professor at the University of North Florida in the counselor education department.

Mrs. Stone is involved in professional organizations. She is President-elect of the Florida Association for Counselor Education and Supervision, Scholarship Chairman for Phi Delta Kappa, Advisor for the First Coast Counseling Association, and is a member of the Florida Counseling Association.

Mrs. Stone married John Douglas Stone August 12, 1972. They reside in Atlantic Beach, Florida, where they are involved in their community.

I certify that I have read this study and that in my opinion it conforms to acceptable standards of scholarly presentation and is fully adequate, in scope and quality, as a dissertation for the degree of Doctor of Education.

Paul George, Chairperson
Professor of Educational Leadership

I certify that I have read this study and that in my opinion it conforms to acceptable standards of scholarly presentation and is fully adequate, in scope and quality, as a dissertation for the degree of Doctor of Education.

James Hensel
Professor of Educational Leadership

I certify that I have read this study and that in my opinion it conforms to acceptable standards of scholarly presentation and is fully adequate, in scope and quality, as a dissertation for the degree of Doctor of Education.

Phillip Clark
Professor of Educational Leadership

I certify that I have read this study and that in my opinion it conforms to acceptable standards of scholarly presentation and is fully adequate, in scope and quality, as a dissertation for the degree of Doctor of Education.

Robert R. Sherman
Professor of Foundations of
Education

I certify that I have read this study and that in my opinion it conforms to acceptable standards of scholarly presentation and is fully adequate, in scope and quality, as a dissertation for the degree of Doctor of Education.

Robert Myrick
Professor of Counselor Education

This dissertation was submitted to the Graduate Faculty of the College of Education and to the Graduate School and was accepted as partial fulfillment of the requirements for the degree of Doctor of Education.

August 1995

_____
Dean, College of Education

_____
Dean, Graduate School